MORE

HOW YOU CAN GET MORE CLIENTS, MORE FEES & MORE TIME

FOR ALL PROFESSIONAL SERVICE PROVIDERS
– ACCOUNTANTS, SOLICITORS, COACHES,
CONSULTANTS, AND SERVICE CONTRACTORS

Paul Davis

Published by OAK TREE PRESS, Cork, Ireland
www.oaktreepress.com / www.SuccessStore.com

© 2016 Paul Davis

A catalogue record of this book is available from the British Library.

ISBN 978 1 78119 217 7 (Paperback)

CONTENTS

BUILDING A STEADY STREAM OF CLIENTS TO YOUR DOOR

ACKNOWLEDGEMENTS

I want to acknowledge all the mentors who I have worked with over the years, for their support and guidance and the ability to learn from other experts.

And for all the business gurus who put their knowledge down in books so that it could be learnt and put into practice by others – thank you.

DEDICATION

This book is dedicated to you, the reader, so that you don't have to go through all the struggles I have had to go through in order to find out what works and what doesn't work when it comes to building a successful business as a professional service provider. Here's to your success!

BONUS TRAINING VIDEO

I have put together a private video tutorial, just for readers of this book, that will help you to apply in your business the strategies I've covered and to fast-track your success to getting more clients, more fees and finally freeing yourself up to do all the extra things you want to get done in life.

You can get this free bonus training video at: **www.davisbusinessconsultants.com/bonus**.

INTRODUCTION

Hello and welcome.

As you read this book and work through the structured exercises, you will discover how easy it is to turn your dreams into realities and your passions into profits, which will put you on the fast-track to your professional success.

This will result in you making more money, more easily and more often and becoming financially independent, allowing you the freedom to do what you choose.

In fact ... because you have taken the first step to work through this book, you are therefore part of an elite group of people committed to personal and professional success and achievement.

People of your calibre usually have a ferocious curiosity for learning. They are looking to maximise their earning potential, create greater fulfilment in life and make a difference by contributing on a grander scale.

Because of your commitment to excellence, you are likely to have an accurate sense of both your strengths and the areas where you can improve, and therefore you are on the path to achieving success in your business faster than ever before.

Working as a service provider, whether you're an accountant, solicitor, consultant, coach, service contractor, trainer, can be exciting, stimulating and financially rewarding. It can lead to a life of permanent learning, constant involvement in challenging projects and a great feeling of accomplishment. And it can lead to working fewer hours for greater financial rewards.

The choice is yours. Where it leads you, is up to you. My guarantee is to give you as many tools, strategies and focus as I can so you can become a highly successful service provider.

Your commitment, if you choose, is to give it 100% as you work through and implement everything in this book.

Firstly ... let me tell you a bit about myself.

I'm Paul Davis, a management accountant and a certified management consultant, and since establishing my own business, **Davis Business Consultants**, I've worked with hundreds of businesses, many of them providing professional services like you.

In order to guarantee results for my clients, I developed a system that has had a high success rate.

I've turned every loss-making company I've worked with into profit. One, a national retailer, had losses of €500k, which I helped turn into a €2m a year profit.

Another, a manufacturing and construction company had €450k losses, which I helped turn into a €750k profit.

Other businesses, in their own words, were "stuck". The business owner was working 60+ hours a week and not achieving the results they really wanted. I helped these business owners achieve a profit growth of 20%+ and, most importantly, taught them the skills and tools they needed to sustain long-term profitable growth.

Clients who I've worked with in the professional services industry (consultants, coaches, solicitors, accountants, trainers, solo-professionals) have achieved increases in fee income of 274%.

And, on a personal note, my clients also told me that they finally felt that they were in complete control of their businesses and they no longer had to work crazy hours to keep the business going. They finally achieved their original goals of more freedom and earning more money.

So you see, I know what really works and what has been proven.

And why am I telling you this?

Well, when I first started my career, I learned how to become a management accountant. It's a great qualification, don't get me wrong. But, like so many other professions, what it didn't teach me was how to develop a business for myself and how to get a steady stream of clients coming to my door.

So I decided to develop my own career path by going into every type of industry sector, working closely with the business owners and running their businesses. I've worked with all types of businesses across national retailers, professional services, construction, manufacturing, designers ... and more.

I've learned how they all did business – what worked and what didn't work. And having worked with so many business owners, I believe there should be more successful businesses. How businesses are run and the methodologies for making them profitable is universal, no matter what industry you're in.

I've been mentored by the best of the best in the USA, UK, Europe and Australia, when it comes to marketing both online and offline and building businesses at a rapid rate. And to those mentors, I am extremely grateful.

I decided a long time ago when managing other businesses to find out for myself what really works and what doesn't work. And over a 10-year period, and a lot of money invested, I brought together the best techniques, tools and strategies that specifically work for professional services. I've honed these skills and techniques based on my own success and that of my clients. For the past number of years, I've presented to audiences of professional service providers in both Ireland and the UK to teach them these techniques. And now I've included them here in this book for you to help you with your business.

My belief is that there is plenty of business out there for everybody. There's trillions of euro and pounds and dollars circulating in the world every day, so there's plenty for everybody and the best way of getting your fair share of those trillions is to help other people to be successful. There are loads of opportunities out there for everybody; you just have to be open to grabbing them.

So I want to teach you everything you need to know to make your business a success and put you well on the path to becoming a successful service provider.

If you're the kind that doesn't like 'networking', that's fine, as this book is about putting systems in place so as to reduce the amount of time you have to spend networking. It's about attracting the kind of clients you want to be working with.

Personally I'm what others would classify as an introvert. Being an introvert, the sheer thought of walking into a room full of people I don't know sends my blood pressure up. As a result, I had to find a way that I could attract clients to me for the services I offered rather than attending networking meeting after another, and being disappointed with the meagre results they can bring.

The system that I'm going to outline in this book achieves a way that you can attract a steady stream of the profitable clients to your door that you want to work with, thereby freeing you up to do what you love doing and using your expertise.

If you don't like selling, then this book is for you. If you've tried advertising and other ways to market your business but didn't get the results you expected, then this book is for you.

The only thing I'll ask you to do is to give it 100%. Everything in this book is there for a reason. Even if you've been working as a service provider for years, it doesn't matter.

Whether you're a solo-professional, working in partnership or part of a large professional firm, start at the very beginning and work through each of the exercises even if you think they don't seem relevant to you right now.

Each exercise is connected to others. If you skip one of the exercises, you're going to lose out later. More importantly, I've added in little gems of information. If you're ready, you'll be able to find these hidden gems that will really make a significant difference to your business. By you giving 100%, you'll get everything from this book that will guarantee your success.

I wish you every success for your future and would be delighted to learn about your progress and achievements from working through this book.

Here's to your success!

Paul

Paul Davis FCMA FIMCA CGMA

BUILDING THE
FOUNDATIONS

THE DECISION TO SET UP AS A SERVICE PROVIDER ...

People choose careers for many reasons but very few such choices result in a smooth satisfying path, right up to retirement. Reality is often very different from the expectations created in our own minds.

The number of people who dream of being their own boss is very large. The number who take active steps to achieve it is very much smaller, and smaller still is the number who actually get there and achieve success!

Fortunately, success is not determined by statistics but by commitment and persistence.

If you're going to start your own professional services business, do it properly and plan the jump. Look at the opportunities open to you, prepare your resources and make your business plan a good one. You must know where your clients will come from and be able to see at least a year ahead.

When you do a good job, you will probably develop twice as much business as you expect. If you can help people and businesses to grow, they will do the same for you. Indeed, if you succeed in delighting them, there will not be enough hours in the day.

If this sounds rather too optimistic, let me redress the balance.

SELF-EMPLOYMENT IS NOT FOR EVERYONE ...

The simple fact is that not everybody is cut out to be his or her own boss. Fortunately, most of those who would never make it would never dare to try.

If you worry about the opinion of others ... do not start your own business.

If the prospect of risk and uncertainty makes you reach for the Valium ... do not start your own business.

If your partner in life is of a nervous disposition ... do not start your own business.

Being your own boss is hard and it will not work if you have anything less than a 100% commitment to making it work. That is where those who have a choice in the matter have a distinct advantage.

The very freedom of action that is such an attractive feature of independence is also the first source of strain. Few people can move from the structured environment of company employment into their own business, without feeling a disorientating sense of detachment and loneliness.

The ability to discuss problems with colleagues, to refer to a higher authority when in doubt, or even the simple pleasure of communal grumbling – all of these are lost.

In their place is a silent, empty vacuum in which your own doubts can grow to be monstrous and your own opinion, however wrong-headed, is the only one available. Unless you have a clear sense of personal direction, the loss of professional association can be deeply disturbing.

Undoubtedly, the biggest pressure on the new practitioner is to maintain a cash flow. After the security of a 'guaranteed' monthly salary, self-employment can be a series of very sharp lessons in how to cope with potentially terminal problems.

The key to surviving self-employment is to enjoy it. Monetary success alone is not enough to enable you to put up with the strain of a job into which you must invest every ounce of your emotional energy. The strain can serve you well or ill. A secure family life is probably the best insurance against taking yourself and your profession too seriously!

Do not consider being an independent service provider unless you are prepared to learn a wealth of skills. Otherwise, it will be a tough road. If you are prepared to face the challenge, the rewards can be totally different; more rewarding and a more flexible lifestyle to that experienced as an employee.

Becoming an independent service provider because it was the default option to avoid finding another job (or not being able to find one at all) is a first-class recipe to tasting disaster. If you do survive the culture shock, it will take you two to three years longer to adapt than if you approach the decision positively.

Carry out **Exercise 1** to determine the factors that are influencing your decision to set up as an independent service provider. There are no right answers to this exercise. But you need to be clear on the reasons why you are setting up in business in the first place.

Remember, your motivation determines your goals. You are what you want to be.

Exercise 1 – Why I Want to Become Independent

	Tick ✓
Use my interpersonal skills	
Be rich	
Intellectual challenge	
Flexible lifestyle	
No commuting	
No other option / Redundant	
Health reasons	
To pay less tax	
I like selling	

Any other reasons? List them out.

TIMING THE DECISION ...

There are of course, two specific times to make the decision to become an independent service provider:

- When you want to jump;
- When you are being pushed.

Looking at the voluntary option:

- Unless you have existing clients / contract work, it can take at least two years to set up a professional practice to replace your current income level;
- €10,000 is not an unrealistic figure for setting up office equipment and facilities;
- Age is not a factor, as the average age of practitioners at start-up is 45;
- Your family / friends / colleagues must be supportive.

The ideal time is when you have been networking for some years and perhaps established a part-time client base. But, of course this can be difficult from the position of full-time employment. Alternatively, you may have obtained a specific contract. But you will have to go back to the 'start', sooner or later, when the contract ends.

Being pushed or 'forced' into becoming an independent service provider:

- Requires even more planning (in a short period of time) than evolving a voluntary career change;
- Means both emotion and financial resources may be limited. You might 'look back in anger' – but this can be either a positive or a negative emotion;
- Means you tell your friends of your situation, but never your clients.

In any event, we will go through the major decisions surrounding:

- What services will you provide?
- In what market will you operate?

It is crucial to recognise that you are fundamentally changing a lifestyle and establishing a business. Perhaps from ground zero.

SETTING UP AN OFFICE (AT HOME OR ELSEWHERE) ...

Firstly ... forget about the plant!

By this, I mean there's many a professional who sets up in practice, buys all the executive furniture, equipment and even the plant for the corner of the office.

And now that the office is set up ... it's time to start looking for clients. Wrong!

Do it the other way around and don't waste your money. Conserve as much of your cash as possible. You can always celebrate each time you get a new client by buying a piece of furniture or equipment.

You've got a choice whether to set up an office from home or elsewhere. However, there are advantages as well as disadvantages with both.

The advantages of working from home include:

- Lower costs;
- No commuting;
- Family back-up.

The disadvantages of working from home include:

- Getting involved in 'domestic' chores;
- Keeping disciplined;
- Image to clients.

The mirror image of these naturally applies to separate 'professional' office accommodation.

Take some time and work through **Exercise 2** and reflect on the right decision for you.

Exercise 2 – Setting Up An Office

Advantages of working from home:

Disadvantages of working from home:

Where would I set up at home?

What things do I need to do to set up the office – phone lines, Internet access, moving furniture?

Whatever your location or address; your business must have its own space. You need to be able to walk away from your desk with the knowledge that everything will be there in its place when you come back and that the dog hasn't run off with your latest client proposal!

Not only that ... you may have been used to meeting other people where you worked previously. This may have been in the office next door or at the 'water station'.

For many professionals, setting up a practice and 'going it alone' can be extremely daunting and lonely. It is worth examining your own personality type to see whether you prefer working with other people, whether you get your energy from working with people or whether you prefer to be alone to think things through. If you are the type that works best with interaction and stimulation from other people, then you may find it best to be located in an office with other business people around you – for example, in a shared office environment.

Another culture shock for professionals starting off is that they no longer can ring the IT department and get their computer sorted out when it crashes, or ring Admin when they run out of paper. Everything comes back to you! Where before you may have worked in a situation where there were plenty of staff around and all you had to do was make a phone call and it was done; now it's a case of you being the one to arrange for something to be done, organise it, supervise it and sometimes even have to carry it out yourself. Even down to cleaning your own office and emptying the bins! For many, this can be extremely difficult, especially if you're coming from a highly paid position and level of authority.

However, there is light at the end of the tunnel, and the quicker you work through this book and start to implement the exercises, the quicker you'll be on your way to building a professional and successful business.

SELF-EMPLOYED OR LIMITED LIABILITY?

A question that I often get asked by service providers is whether to set up as a self-employed individual or in the form of a limited company.

The answer is ... it depends!

Pointers to take into account include:

- Who your target market is and whether the VAT laws affect them differently – for example, will you be dealing with companies (which usually can recover VAT) or with individuals (who generally can't)?
- How big you want to build your business;
- How your competitors are established;
- How it will affect your business image;
- Whether you plan to sell the business at some point in the future.

There are so many questions to be asked and answered, and the best advice I can give you at this point is to seek professional advice. There are different legal and tax laws that come into play in different countries and each individual's situation is different.

Talk to friends who have a professional service business and ask them what has worked for them and what they would do if they were to start all over again.

Listen to them, but don't necessarily take their advice. Many a time people will suggest that you do what they did so that it confirms in their own mind that they made the right decision themselves. So you may not be getting the best advice.

Once you have that knowledge, talk to an accountant. And if need be, talk to a number of accountants, as some accountants will have different opinions.

When you're armed with all the information, pros and cons, then you're in a position to make a decision.

INSURANCE ...

Without question, if you're going to provide a professional service – you need to take out Professional Indemnity Insurance (or PII).

Have you got your home or your car insured? Then why wouldn't you take out PI insurance for your business?

If a client ever made a claim against you for bad advice or their system crashed as a result of something you did to their computer server, or their building collapsed as a result of a mistake in your engineering advice – where will the money come from to pay for it?

Although it may seem like a large fee to pay out when you're starting off, it's a necessity – just like having a computer. Get a number of quotes and contact your professional association as many of them have relationships with insurance companies that offer privileged rates for members. It may not be as expensive as you might think!

If you're serious about building a business, you have to be serious about looking after your clients' interests. You'll also be able to sleep easy at night knowing that you have insurance in place.

ON THE ROAD...

If you've survived going through this book so far – well done!

You're now on the road to building a successful business.

The previous couple of sections can be quite daunting for some people and can even put them off setting up in business in the first place. The fact that you've made it this far means that you stand a great chance of turning your service into a successful business.

So ... why do you want to set up as a professional service provider in the first place?

Some people want to make more money, some people want to make a difference in their environment and economy, some people spot a gap in the market and want to capitalise on it, while others want more freedom and fun and to be away from having a boss.

What is it for you? Complete **Exercise 3** so that you have a record of your reasons.

Take the time to do this exercise. You will need to refer back to it later and it is always good to revisit what you have written when times get tough.

Then next ... we're going to start building the blocks, one on top of the other so as to make sure your foundations are right. This will enable you to get your business on the correct course.

Exercise 3 – Why Do You Want To Be Independent?

The reasons I want to set up as a professional service provider are:

DETERMINING YOUR CORE COMPETENCIES...

Personal core competencies are attributes or things that you do for a business that clearly set you apart from others. In other words, they are skills that make you special and valuable.

And because your competencies are going to be the focus of your career, they have to involve doing something you enjoy. There are several defining characteristics of core competencies.

Core competencies provide access to a wide variety of avenues for you to pursue in your own business. Core competencies are skill sets that you possess. The skills may be learned or innate. They're not values, goals, or objectives, and they do not diminish with use. They are quite different from physical assets that depreciate over time. They are actually enhanced as they are applied and shared. More importantly, they're difficult for your competitors to imitate.

However, if they are not nurtured and protected, competencies fade much like knowledge fades when it is not used. That's why competency building is so important for you.

What is it that you really enjoy doing? What have you been recognised as being excellent at, yet to you, it came with little effort or thought, it came naturally to you.

Now complete **Exercise 4** to define your core competencies.

Exercise 4 – Your Core Competencies

What are my core competencies? What am I really good at, what is it that I really enjoy doing and comes naturally to me?

Now that you know what your core competencies are, let's look at this from a different angle.

I want you to think back to the time you left school.

When you're back at that place in your mind's eye, start to roll the years forward slowly, and as you do, ask yourself to pick out all the times where you achieved something and all the things you enjoyed doing.

This may have been passing a particular exam, getting a qualification, winning an award, securing your first big deal, saving €1,000s for the company you worked for through an initiative you introduced. It doesn't matter what they were, just remember back to each of those events.

On **Exercise 5**, start to write down all your achievements to date.

Exercise 5 – Your Achievements

What have I achieved?

NOW LET'S LOOK AT VALUES ...

Each and every one of us has many personal values. These values are important to us. They are the rules that we live by.

Personal values evolve from circumstances with the external world and some can change over time.

Put simply, values are what are important to us in life.

If you look at your life and there is something that you feel is missing, then take a look at your values and see where that missing item appears in your values.

For example, if you say having money is one of your core values, and yet you don't have much money in your bank account, take a look at your values and see where 'having money' appears in your list of values. Is it number one for you or is there another value that you hold dearly that is contradicting your value for having money? You may find that money is something that you would like to have or aspire to having, but it's not truly a core value for you.

The simple fact is that our values are what drive us. However deep down within us, if there is a value that is not being met, we can have a sense that everything is just not right. It is important that you find out what your values are as this will focus you on what is important to you and what really deep down you are passionate about. Complete **Exercise 6** to determine your values.

If you are having difficulty completing this values exercise, I discuss values in more detail in my other book, *EVOLVE*, which you can find by following this link: **www.thebookevolve.com**.

Exercise 6 – Your Core Values

My core values: What is important to me in life?

GETTING YOUR VISION RIGHT...

Have you got a vision for your business?

By this, I don't mean something that you put together in an 'away day' or have dreamed up with a marketing expert, put in a picture frame and either hang in a prominent position in the reception area or worse still, keep in the bottom drawer of your filing cabinet.

A vision is a statement of where you're trying to bring your business to. It's a picture of what your business will look like in time to come. This might be two years down the track or five years. It's got to be able to paint a picture in your own mind of what you're trying to achieve.

A vision needs to reflect your own core values and what is important to you in your business – it's the main reason why you were passionate about setting up in business in the first place and the difference you want to make in your environment.

Another way of looking at it is to answer these questions:

- What is your ultimate purpose in life?
- What do you want to achieve?
- What legacy do you want to have left behind you?
- What change do you want to make to the world, the economy, the environment?

Whatever it is, only you can determine it. It's something that you feel passionate about and want to achieve. You don't have to believe you'll achieve it yet. That comes later.

Just imagine if there were no barriers to you achieving what it is you want to achieve and would love to achieve, are passionate about and really enjoy, what would it be?

Let's look at an example of a vision from a well-known Irish business owner, Padraig Ó Céidigh of Aer Arann ...

My original vision was to become a safe, reliable, profitable service to the Aran Islands. Then the vision became Ireland's internal airline and now my vision is to become the best regional airline in the world.

As you can see, it's OK for your vision to change over time just like Padraig's did. As you achieve your initial vision, it then becomes necessary to stretch yourself again. Being a true entrepreneur means constantly striving to be the best in your field and evolving as the environment changes. The purpose of having a vision is to have something to aim towards.

When you get into your car and your Sat Nav asks, "Where do you want to go today?", do you give it vague directions in order to point your car in a particular direction? No, I guessed not. Your Sat Nav needs you to punch in the exact address of where you want to go.

A vision acts as the Sat Nav in your brain. The clearer you have the 'address' of where you want to go with your business, the faster and more focused you will be in getting there. And for me, I choose to believe that what you focus on is what you get.

But a vision is not something that you put together and file away. It's much more than that – it's the picture you paint for your staff and everybody that's involved in helping you achieve it. By them knowing where you want to get to, it results in everybody being aligned to your focus and the more aligned everybody is, then the more they can help you achieve it.

A vision is something that you refer to as often as possible in order to make sure you're still on the right path and that everybody is singing off the same hymn sheet.

On 25 May 1961, President John F. Kennedy gave a speech to Congress where he said, "I believe that this nation should commit itself to achieving the goal, before this decade is out, of landing a man on the moon and returning him safely to the Earth".

Everybody thought it wouldn't be possible but it became the birth of something much greater. One reason why President John F. Kennedy put this vision together was to get the whole population out of the recession and get them focused on a higher goal, creating an excitement that stimulated the American economy at a time when it was much needed.

Kennedy's vision became a reality on 20 July 1969, when Apollo 11 commander Neil Armstrong took a small step for himself and a giant leap for humanity.

Another example ... on 29 August 1963, Martin Luther King, Jr. delivered his "I have a dream" speech on the steps of the Lincoln Memorial, where he painted the picture for his America, where he put such clarity on what it would look like.

On 20 January 2009, President Barack Obama was sworn in as 44th President of the United States.

Your personal vision is your first step in determining your strategic plan. By knowing where you want to get to, you can then work back to plan out how you're going to get there.

So for this next exercise, close your eyes (after reading these instructions, of course!) and just dream about where you want to be in, say, three or five years from now. What does your business look like? Look around you. What are the things you see? What are people saying about you? What are the kinds of things you hear around you? What does it feel like? Where are you? Paint as clear a picture in your mind as possible. And remember, there are no limitations. Dream big and let yourself to bring yourself to the vision of where you want to get to.

After about 10 minutes of allowing yourself to dream of that vision, write down as much detail as possible in **Exercise 7** so that you can refer back to it in future and be able to connect with that same vision.

I cover personal vision in more detail in my other book, *EVOLVE*, if you want to find out more about this subject.

Exercise 7 – Your Personal Vision

My personal vision is...

YOUR MISSION...

Simply put, your mission is a statement of:

- What you do;
- Who you serve;
- What you stand for; and
- Why you do what you do.

Having defined your vision, core competencies and values will help you get closer at defining your mission. This is important, as it will help you to define your marketing message later.

Now complete **Exercise 8** to define what your mission is for your business.

Exercise 8 – Your Mission

My mission is...

WHAT'S DIFFERENT ABOUT YOU?

Now that we have looked at your vision, your mission, your values, your core competencies and past achievements, and as you take a look at the exercises you've completed, ask yourself this question: "What's different about me?".

There is always something that is different. Either you have a unique way of solving people's problems or you have a success rate in a particular field. There is something ... but what is it? There's no need to be bashful when it comes to this. If need be, ask somebody else to review what you've put together in the exercises and ask them what they think is different about you.

The reason for doing this is that no matter what field you're in – solicitor, accountant, architect, consultant or coach – there is something extra that will make you different and enable you to stand out from the crowd. There is something that you do exceptionally well or something that you are very passionate about.

You may now begin to see a trend appearing in these exercises. These exercises all come together, as they all work together in helping you to define your market and how you will be able to stand out from the crowd and define a unique blue ocean market for yourself and so find where you're going to make more money.

Now complete **Exercise 9** to find out what's different about you. If you can't think of anything straight away, that's OK.

If need be, just write whatever comes into your head, even if it doesn't make any sense at first. If you hit a blank after a few minutes, that's OK, just keep going. When you've gone through at least two 'blank' moments and written everything that you can think of, then you're finished. And if you still can't think of anything, leave it for a while, ask yourself the same question before you go to bed and over the next few days the answers will come.

Exercise 9 – What's Different About You?

What differentiates me? What do others say that is different about how I work or approach different tasks?

ANALYSIS TIME ...

We're now at a point where we've looked at why you want to set up a professional practice (and if you've already set one up, what was the reason you set it up in the first place – it may have changed since). We've also looked at what it is you enjoy doing, your values, and where you want to get to with your business.

Pretty soon, we're going to look at how we go about marketing yourself and having a flow of clients come to you on a regular basis.

But first ... there's one final piece of analysis work we need to do. And that is to take a look at your external environment as well as at yourself.

You may have come across a PEST and SWOT analysis before. Put simply, a PEST analysis stands for Political, Economic, Social and Technological, while a SWOT analysis stands for Strengths, Weaknesses, Opportunities and Threats.

When we look at a PEST analysis, we're looking at the external environment – what is going on outside. By carrying out this exercise, we take note of different trends that are happening which may alter how we deliver services or whether we are entering into a declining or growing market space. By so doing, you can alter your course of action and make sure you stay on the right course for a growing business.

Examples of **Political** factors that may come into play include:

- Current or future legislation;
- Activities of regulatory bodies;
- Government policies;
- Funding initiatives.

Examples of **Economic** factors might include:

- Home economic growth or decline;

- Overseas economic trends;
- Taxation rates.

Examples of **Social** factors might include:

- Lifestyle trends;
- Demographics;
- Buying patterns.

And **Technological** might include:

- Social networking;
- Future technology trends;
- Consumer buying;
- Innovation.

By looking at these factors, you will be able to future-proof your services, become a market leader with your services and be best placed to ride the wave of the next trend.

Now it's time to complete **Exercise 10** and see what this analysis throws up for you and how you could be different from the crowd in your field.

Exercise 10 – PEST Analysis

My PEST analysis...

Political	Economic

Social	Technological

Now that we've looked at your PEST analysis, it's time to look at your own SWOT analysis, considering your Strengths, Weaknesses, Opportunities and Threats.

Examples of **Strengths** might include:

- Organised;
- Focused;
- Expertise in a particular subject – for example, Taxation;
- Built a previous business.

Examples of personal **Weaknesses** might include:

- Procrastination;
- Poor marketing skills;
- No reputation yet.

Examples of **Opportunities** might include:

- Possible alliances with other partners;
- Availability of student interns to help with setting up;
- Extended personal network.

And **Threats** might include:

- Lack of financial resources to sustain the business;
- Rapid changes in technology or knowledge requirements;
- Health issues.

By doing this exercise, you can begin to do something about your weaknesses – by getting more training or having somebody take care of an area of the business that you are potentially weak at. You also can leverage off your strengths, plan to go after opportunities and recognise any threats that may arise. And if need be, you can put together a plan of action to eliminate any real threats.

By completing **Exercise 11**, you can then prioritise any of the areas that need to be addressed.

Exercise 11 – Your SWOT Analysis

My SWOT analysis...

Personal Strengths	Personal Weaknesses

Personal Opportunities	Personal Threats

When you've completed all the exercises so far, it's now time to stand back and review everything that you have done.

The reason being is that, by completing the exercises, new ideas will appear that you never would have thought about before.

With all this information to hand, you can then decide whether you need to change or tweak your vision or mission by taking on board what has come to light. Make those changes now and then we can move on to the next stage.

Although I'm going to cover how you manage your time at a later stage in this book, there's one area I want to cover now – and that is about setting goals.

The majority of people who set up in business like to get everything done and typically we want to have it done yesterday.

This all seems logical in our own mind. However, when we don't get done all the things we had planned, what happens is that we get into a never-ending spiral of trying to get more done today because the stuff we wanted to get done yesterday didn't happen, and not only that but our stress levels begin to rise and we start to beat ourselves up in our head.

But typically ... some of the reasons we set up in business were to have more freedom, be our own boss and work less hours, and here we are working longer hours and getting more stressed as the days go by.

In my experience in dealing with professional business owners, there's one main factor to successfully achieving your goals, and that's properly planning out what you want to achieve and being realistic in your expectations.

Having completed the exercises so far, taking into account where you want to bring the business to, if you were to set just three goals for your business, what would they be?

Now setting goals is an art in itself and if you've never set goals before, now is the time to start. By setting goals, you'll immediately put yourself in the top percentage among successful people who do. In setting your goals, use the acronym SMART, which stands for **S**pecific, **M**easurable, **A**chievable, **R**elevant and **T**imely.

Let's look at an example:

I want to have a website up and running.

Now you can see straight away where this goal falls down in each of the characteristics of being a SMART goal.

If we were to turn this goal into:

I'm going to have a four page brochure-type website for my business up and running by 31 July whereby I'll have received three enquiries through my website.

How different is that?

- It's very **specific** – four page brochure-type website;
- It's **measurable** – three enquiries;
- **Achievable** – if there are six months to 31 July, then, yes, it's achievable; if there is only one month, then perhaps not;
- **Relevant** – it's a website that's going to promote the business;
- **Timely** – there's a timeframe to achieve this goal by 31 July.

You get the idea?

Now in **Exercise 12**, set three goals that you want to achieve for your business and ensure they're SMART goals.

Exercise 12 – Your Goals

Three things I want to achieve in my business are:

SMART Goal 1

SMART Goal 2

SMART Goal 3

Now that you've set your three goals, it's time to plan how they're going to be achieved. A lot of the time people set a goal with the expectation that they'll achieve it but they haven't looked at how it's going to be done. (This may not be you but I'm sure you know other people that do that.)

So what are all the things that need to be done in order to achieve this goal?

If we take the example used earlier of the website, items to be done might include:

- Secure a web designer;
- Register a domain name;
- Decide on the layout of the website;
- Decide on the four page headings;
- Compile the wording for each of the four pages;
- Agree the design and colour scheme;
- Test the website functionality;
- Make the website live;
- Update business cards and stationery.

These are just some of the items that might need to be done.

On **Exercise 13**, write in your goal on the top of the page. There's a separate page for each goal. List out all the different items that need to be done in order to achieve the particular goal.

Once you have that done, fill in how long you think each of those items will take to complete. You can refer to the sample that I've included to see how a finished plan might look like for your goals.

Exercise 13 – Plan For Your Goals

Sample Goal: I'm going to have a four page brochure type website for my business up and running by the 31st July whereby I'll have received three enquiries through my website.

Sample Plan for Sample Goal

W/e = week ended date

Action to be taken	W/e 08/5	W/e 15/5	W/e 22/5	W/e 29/5	W/e 05/6	W/e 12/6	W/e 19/6	W/e 26/6	W/e 03/7	W/e 10/7	W/e 17/7	W/e 24/7	W/e 31/7
Secure a web designer	X												
Register a domain name	X												
Decide on the layout of the website		X	X	X									
Decide on the four page headings					X								
Compile the wording for each of the pages						X	X	X					
Agree the design and colour scheme									X	X			
Test the website and functionality											X	X	
Make the website live												X	
Update business cards and stationery													X

Goal 1: _____

Plan for Goal 1

Action to be taken	W/e	W/e	W/e	W/e	W/e	W/e	W/e	W/e	W/e	W/e	W/e	W/e	W/e

Goal 2: _____

Plan for Goal 2

Action to be taken	W/e	W/e	W/e	W/e	W/e	W/e	W/e	W/e	W/e	W/e	W/e	W/e	W/e

Goal 3: _____

Plan for Goal 3

Action to be taken	W/e	W/e	W/e	W/e	W/e	W/e	W/e	W/e	W/e	W/e	W/e	W/e	W/e

What you might find is that the date that you had set at the beginning may need to be pushed out as you realise that, with all the tasks that need to be done, as well as doing everything else in your business, it's not possible to get it done by the initial planned date.

That's OK and it's better to realise that now, rather than getting to the date and beating yourself because you didn't achieve the goal within the timeframe you first thought.

By doing this simple exercise in everything you do with your business, you'll find that your stress levels will be greatly lowered and you'll begin to enjoy your business a lot more.

Everything can't be done at the same time and by tomorrow!

BUILDING A STEADY STREAM OF CLIENTS TO YOUR DOOR

BUILDING YOUR CLIENT BASE ...

Now that you've started building a solid foundation for your business, it's time to look at how you're going to maintain an ongoing steady stream of clients, who hold you in high esteem and want the service that you provide.

Some of the exercises that you've already done from the previous section will give you a lot of the information you now need to complete this section.

First, you need to identify your target market.

YOUR TARGET MARKET ...

Your target market is made up of a specific group of people that have similar characteristics, and therefore have similar needs and wants and so they buy similar services.

When you look back over your career and your business to date, and all the people you came in contact with in your professional life, who were the people you most enjoyed working with? What were the industry sectors you really got a buzz from?

No matter what service you provide, there will always be a sector that you have an underlying passion for.

For example, if you're a solicitor, you may have a passion or interest in the restaurant sector, or you may like working in the aircraft industry. If you're an accountant, you may like working with solicitors or coaches or the haulage industry.

Think long and hard about this as it's your first critical step to being really successful in your business.

Make a list of all the employment positions you had, hobbies you took up, people you enjoyed helping in the past, communities, organisations, businesses and so on.

Go to **Exercise 14** and list all these out and mark the ones you really enjoyed the most.

Exercise 14 – Industry Sectors You Enjoy

List out all the industry sectors, groups, businesses, careers, you've worked with up to now, hobbies and interests. Then mark the ones you really enjoyed working with the most.

What you'll find after doing this exercise is that there'll be a common thread running through each of them. It may be a particular sector that you like working with or have a passion for, or it may be a type of individual you like working with.

No matter what it is, there will always be a trend. Whether it's today or over the next number of weeks that you discover this trend, that's OK.

If there is more than one sector that comes to light in this exercise, start by eliminating the ones you least want to work with.

It is best to only have one sector in mind when doing the rest of the exercises in this section. When you have your marketing to that sector working well and it's bringing in a lot of business, you can always go back over the exercise again and pick another sector to work with.

Now that you have the particular industry sector in mind, let's clearly identify this industry with more details. Go to **Exercise 15** and start to put their characteristics together.

The important thing is that you enjoy working with this particular sector. You'll only be successful if you enjoy what you're doing.

When you've completed **Exercise 15**, let's check if it's the right sector for you and whether there is potential for your business to grow through that sector.

By completing **Exercise 16**, you will have a better idea as to whether this is a sector for you to concentrate on. It's better to find this out now rather than waste hundreds of hours and €000s pursuing a sector that in the long run is not right for you.

Exercise 15 – Your Target Industry Characteristics

What is my target market / what is the sector I want to work in and enjoy working with?

Who / what are they?

Where are they?

Exercise 16 – Is This Sector Right For You?

Why do I want to work with this sector?

What do I like about this sector?

What do I not like about this sector?

What do I know about this sector?

What expertise, qualifications, experience do I have in working with this sector?

How big is this sector? / How many potential clients are there?

Is this sector a growing / declining sector?

What threats / changes do I see happening for the growth of this sector?

If, based on your answers to this exercise, you find that it's not the right sector for you to work with, that's OK. Just go back to **Exercise 14**, pick the next industry on your list and re-do **Exercise 16**.

Now let's refine your target market a bit more. Out of the sector that you've just identified that you want to work with, and that you really enjoy working with, let's identify your ideal client. These clients will have specific characteristics within the sector that you've just described.

Have a look at **Exercise 17** and work through describing what your *ideal* client looks like from that sector. It's not to say that you wouldn't work with the entire group of people in that sector. Let's just look at the scenario if you were to describe a perfect working day for you, what would be the ideal client you would most want to spend that day with.

Some of their characteristics might be:

- How long they have been in business;
- Whether they are male or female;
- Whether they are of a particular age bracket;
- Whether they come from a particular background;
- Whether their business is of a particular size;
- How many employees they have;
- Geographically where they are located.

Now that you have your ideal client in mind and a clear description of what they're like, you can be more focused about your approach to target that market.

It's not to say that you'll only deal with your ideal client, but if you are specific about the type of client you want and enjoy working with, then you'll be more focused on picking them out of the crowd and more focused in attracting them to you.

Exercise 17 – Your Ideal Client

My ideal client is...

WILLIAM TELL ...

Do you remember the story of William Tell?

According to legend, William Tell was an expert with a bow and arrow and lived in the mountains of Switzerland.

At the time, William Tell's home in Switzerland was under the control of Austria and a ruler named Gessler, who thought that he was so important that the citizens should salute him even when he wasn't there. So, he put his hat on a pole in the centre of the town and commanded the citizens to bow down to it.

William Tell arrived in town one day with his son and refused to salute the hat. Gessler was very upset, but instead of killing William Tell right there, he challenged him to shoot an arrow at an apple that was placed on his son's head. If he succeeded, William Tell could remain free.

William Tell did shoot the apple off his son's head with a single arrow. But Gessler noticed that before he tried, Tell had taken two arrows out of his quiver and so asked him why. William Tell answered, "If I had missed, that second arrow would have been headed your way".

The purpose of telling this story is to see whether you would prefer to target your marketing at your ideal clients with a shotgun or a laser rifle? Many service providers approach the market using a shotgun approach. A lot of them waste €000s on advertising, and hundreds of hours of their time chasing after a multitude of possible prospects. Many of them give up in the end and resign themselves to being continuously in the battle of chasing clients (more on that later!).

What makes a successful service provider successful is their laser focus approach to the market.

The more focused you are in aiming at your prospects, the more successful you'll become, and much faster.

YOUR NICHE ...

What you've just worked through in **Exercise 17** is your 'niche' market. This is where you'll begin to use your laser focus and begin to shine in the marketplace. You'll become the expert in your field specific for your target market.

What this enables you to do is to stand out from the crowd. Coupled with that, you'll be doing it in a sector that you have a passion for and you'll be working with people you enjoy working with. How great is that?

You may find that you want to have a few niche markets, and that's OK. For now, we're going to just concentrate on one particular niche and really make that one work first before moving on to the others.

The biggest concern that many professionals have when I mention focusing on a niche is: *"But what about all the other potential clients. Am I not going to be missing out on them?"*. This is a legitimate concern. However, you need to keep in mind that you won't be cutting off all the other potential business from coming to you.

Think of it this way – you probably have your favourite local restaurant that you go to regularly. When you sit down at the table and browse through the menu, there's usually one dish that you prefer most, but that doesn't stop you from having a look at all the others. And sometimes you might choose a different dish depending on your mood, but most of the time you'll pick your 'old reliable'. While you're focused on your niche, there is nothing stopping you from working with other types of clients as they come your way. Even though I have a few niches that I focus on for my business, I've also had clients come to me who were outside my target niches – funeral directors, bakers, restaurants, courier companies, and others. Nothing stopped me from working with these clients as I knew I could help them, but I didn't stop focusing on my niche.

SO WHY IS FOCUS SO IMPORTANT?

What you need to understand is that your mind operates a bit like an Internet search engine. If you enter the phrase "any business" into Google (as so many professionals effectively do), what you get back is over 3.5 billion results.

Your mind can't process that many. When you ask somebody to refer 'any business' to you, their mind can't process that either.

However, if you enter 'petroleum companies' into Google, you get back about 119 million results – a bit more manageable. However, when you start to think about petroleum companies, you can start to make a list of all the companies that you know. If you ask people for a referral to a 'petroleum company', they too will be able to think of such a company far easier and quicker than if you ask them for 'any business'.

Let's take the example of petroleum companies a bit further. If you do that search on Google, appearing on page one is a list of all petroleum companies, from the largest to the smallest, the associations that look after petroleum companies, and if you go further you will find a list of members, conferences that are held for petroleum companies, magazines and industry specific reports. All of this will come into relevance as we move through the exercises in the rest of this book, but I want you to see that it is a lot easier to build a business when you're focused on a target.

The next thing you should know is that you want to build your business and be known for something. The best way you can do this is to focus on a niche.

When you think of Disney movies and what you will get from a Disney movie, you begin to list out things like fun, fantasy, fairytale, good and evil, happy ending, memorable songs, a teaching told as a story and so on. Ultimately Disney movies are known for 'family entertainment'. This means that no matter what Disney movie you put on to watch in front of your family – young children, parents, grandparents – there will be no embarrassing moments to watch and everybody will be uplifted by the end of the movie.

That's what Disney movies are known for. What is it that you want to be known for in your industry?

Let's take another couple of examples of companies that have focused on a niche market.

Take Ben & Jerry's ice cream. They focus on creating new and wonderful flavoured ice creams, from peanut butter, to cheesecake, to cookie dough, and the list goes on and on. They make ice cream for people who want to try different flavours. They don't just make vanilla, strawberry, mint and chocolate ice cream like all the other manufacturers of ice cream.

Now does this prevent anybody from having a Ben & Jerry's ice cream? The answer is "No". But their business focus, marketing and product development is for that target market that wants to try different flavoured ice creams.

Let's take another example – Harley-Davidson motorcycles. If you were to describe the target market for Harley-Davidson when they first established, you would come up with an ideal client along the lines of male, middle aged, mid-life crisis, likes wearing shades, leather jacket and trousers, wants freedom, and has a beard.

That's the ideal client they had targeted. They weren't going after the commuter or run-around bike market like so many other manufacturers. They knew their target market: people that wanted to express themselves, had a lot of money to spend and wanted quality.

If you think about Harley-Davidson now – does it prevent anybody in the market for a motorcycle from considering buying a Harley? The answer again is "No". Whether you're a male, female, mid-20s or mid-80s, you will still more than likely take a look at a Harley when you come across it and perhaps secretly want to take it for a ride.

If you pick a niche and get known for what you do within that niche, it won't prevent anybody else from requesting your services. And it doesn't prevent you from deciding whether you want to work with a client from any other industry or not.

The key is that you want to get known as an expert in what you do for that niche.

YOUR SALES FUNNEL ...

OK, so now that you have specified your market sector and identified your ideal client, the next thing we need to work out is how many clients you wish to have. We do this by a process that determines how many people you need to be talking to in order to achieve the level of revenue you're targeting. This is called your 'sales funnel'.

So, for example, if you want to be working with, say, 10 clients, you may need to be talking to 100 prospects on a regular basis.

Imagine an orchard where you're growing apple trees to make cider. If it takes 2 kg of apples to make 1 litre of cider, and you want to produce 1,000 litres of cider, then how many apple trees will you need to plant to make 1,000 litres of cider? Well, 1,000 litres of cider requires 2,000 kgs of apples, and if each tree can produce an average of 19 kgs of apples, then you will need to plant at least 105 trees. But some of the apples will be lost along the way of processing, some will be rotten, some won't grow into a full apple and some trees may die. So you need to plant more than 105 trees to allow for all this.

Your sales funnel operates in the same way and your prospects follow the same route as the apples take. You need to plant more trees, meaning you need to be in contact with a lot more prospects in order to turn a certain number of them into clients.

Have a look at **Exercise 18** and work through the equations in order to find out how many people you need to be talking to on a regular basis so that you can achieve your target fee income. I've included sample figures in the chart so that you can follow the formulas.

Exercise 18 – Your Sales Funnel

My sales funnel...

Criteria	Example	My Company Revenue Stream 1	My Company Revenue Stream 2	My Company Revenue Stream 3
What is your sales target for the year	€99,000			
What is the *average* monthly fee that you receive from a client	€500			
On Average how many months do you receive that *average* monthly fee	6			
What is the total value that client is worth to you (in our example multiply €500 x 6 = €3,000)	€3,000			

My sales funnel continued...

Therefore how many *average* total client values do you need, to meet your sales target (in our example divide €99,000 / €3,000 = 33)	33
How many prospect client meetings or proposals do you need to have in order to win one client (e.g. 1 in 3?)	3
How many prospect client meetings or proposals do you need to have in order to reach the number of new clients that you need (in our example multiply 33 x 3)	99
How many leads do you need to have, in order to achieve one prospect meeting or get to make one proposal (e.g. 1 meeting out of 10 leads?, therefore in our example multiply 99 x 10 = 990)	990

The final figure (in our example being 990) – this is the number of leads you need to generate on average in order for you to reach your target sales figure for the year. What is the figure for you?

ADD A ZERO ...

So you see ... now you know how many people you need to aim towards.

A lot of service providers when they're looking for clients focus on the number of clients they want – perhaps 10 clients.

However, what many forget is that they need to be focusing on a much greater number, say 100, in order for the funnel to turn into 10 clients.

But I want to bring you one step further.

Imagine there are two people standing in front of you, and they are standing about five feet apart, facing each other. Between them they're holding one end of a rope each. They're holding the rope horizontally 10 feet above the ground between them.

Now, in order to get over the rope, what are all the ways you could try?

Some suggestions might be: jump over it, get a ladder, stand on a box, get somebody to lift you over ... Make a note of any other suggestions that you might have to get over the rope before moving on to the next paragraph.

Now, imagine the rope has been moved so that, instead of it being 10 feet from the ground, it is now 100 feet from the ground. What ways would you need to try in order to get over the rope now?

Again some suggestions might be: get a longer ladder, fly over it, parachute over it, use a cherry-picker, use a fire-engine ladder, hire a crane, take an elevator, build scaffolding ... List any other suggestions that you can think of to get over the rope that is now 100 feet above the ground.

Now take a look at the second set of suggestions.

What you'll find is that all the suggestions in the second list – to get over the rope 100 feet above the ground – including the ones you came up with yourself, also apply to the first example of where you had to get over the rope that was only 10 feet above the ground.

Yes? You see, when you look at a target to get 10 clients, all you think about are the options you have to get those 10 clients.

What I'm going to ask you to do is to add a zero to whatever figure you calculated in your sales funnel. So if your target figure was 300, I want you to add a zero to the figure, so it becomes 3,000.

It doesn't matter whether you add the zero to your fee income target or to your client prospects target. Try them all and see what happens.

At first, you may think it would be difficult to get 3,000. But just think about it for a while and let it settle. Don't put any limitations or constraints on your capabilities. The resources can always be worked out later. For now, just think of all the strategies or ideas that come to mind when you add a zero to your sales funnel figure.

What you'll find is that it opens up a myriad of new possibilities in your mind. You might partner with others, build joint venture relationships, deliver your service in a completely different way and / or choose to build your service in a new geographic market. Whatever ideas come to mind as to what you would need to do in order to reach the new target, write them all down. When you think bigger in these ways, you will find that it will open you up to other possibilities. And remember all of these possibilities you can use for your lower target anyway!

While you're imagining this, go to **Exercise 19** and write down whatever ideas, possibilities, actions, strategies that you come up with.

Exercise 19 – Adding A Zero

When I add a zero to my target, the ideas, possibilities, actions, strategies that I can come up with are...

WHAT DO THEY WANT?

OK, so you have identified your market and all the possibilities that have been opened to you as a result of the last exercise. Now you need to find out what your target market wants.

Many professionals spend their time putting together their shopping list of all the services they can provide in the hope that somebody will identify with one of those services and come along to buy it.

BIG mistake. This is where €000s are lost all the time. So I want to save you this pain and money.

People only tune into one radio station: WIIFM – What's In It For Me! Your prospects don't want to hear about you, how great you are and what you can provide. They only want to know what benefits they obtain from engaging your services.

Now this is an easy shift for you, because you've already identified your target market. It's one that you have experience in, are passionate about and have a lot of knowledge of.

So put yourself into the mind-set of your client and think about what they truly want by imagining their situation.

Back a number of years ago, a film was released called, *What Women Want*, starring Mel Gibson and Helen Hunt. You might have seen the movie yourself and, if you haven't, it's worth renting a copy. It's a good comedy where Nick Marshall (Mel Gibson) gets a whole new outlook on life when a fluke accident gives him the ability to read women's minds. At first, this 'gift' provides Nick with way too much information, but he begins to realise that he can use it to good effect, especially when it comes to outwitting his new boss, Darcy Maguire (Helen Hunt). It's a great laugh watching the happenings that go on. But here's the thing, Nick Marshall had the ability to know what the little voice was saying that chatters away in the heads of the women he was around. We all know that little voice, we all have one. Sometimes it's a positive voice, but oftentimes it's negative, picking up our faults and telling us what we're no good at. Do you know this voice? Or is it just me who has that negative little voice!

Anyway, getting back to the movie, there is also a sub-plot – where Erin, the company secretary, is contemplating suicide and all her thoughts are about how worthless she is, how she's invisible to those around her. Then one day, when Erin doesn't appear in the office, Nick goes looking for her and finds her in her apartment.

You see there are times when we will be at our lowest. It could be during the day when stress levels are high, or it can be during the 'witching hour', that time in the middle of the night when we can't sleep because of all the thoughts that are going on in our head. We have a conversation with ourselves trying to figure out a solution to our problems. Just as Nick was able to 'hear' what the little voice was saying inside Erin's head, we need to imagine what the little voice is saying inside our potential client's head.

It's these scenarios that you need to imagine for your clients. What are they thinking? What conversation is going on in their head? What are their worries and concerns? What language are they using? For example, a business owner who is worrying about where he's going to get the money to pay the staff wages will be saying "Where will I get the money from?", "Where can I get more business?", "What can I do to get more cash in?", and so on. He will use simple language, not the latest buzzwords like 'organisational development', or 'restructuring' or 'team development'. That's not the language of that little voice. So what you have to keep in mind when doing this exercise is the conversation that is going on for your target clients when they are thinking about the problems that they have.

With that in mind, work through **Exercise 20** and write down what your target clients' pains and wants are.

Exercise 20 – What Do They Want?

What do they want?

What do they desire?

What problems do they want solved?

What are their pains?

What keeps them awake at night?

What / who are they angry about?

What frustrates them?

What do they need?

What prevents them from getting what they want?

What knowledge / skills / experience / successes do I have that would help them achieve their goals and overcome their obstacles?

It's easy isn't it?

And it makes a big difference when you look at it from your clients' perspective. Now you can see how your marketing message is going to be different, and how it's going to connect with your potential clients.

YOUR USP ...

Now I want to take you back to an exercise that you did earlier, **Exercise 9**.

This was where you worked out what is different about you. From a marketing perspective, the more you can differentiate yourself from the crowd of professionals in your field, the more successful you'll be.

Imagine if you're an accountant and you go along to a networking meeting where, on the attendance list, you see there are six other accountants in the room.

What's going to be different about you compared to the other six accountants in the room?

In marketing-speak, we call this your Unique Selling Proposition (USP). It aims to identify what is unique about you, your business, how you approach the market, how you do things.

Your USP is made up of a number of different elements:

- Your name;
- What you do;
- Who you do it for (target niche);
- What's different or unique about you;
- The value / results you provide.

It's also part of your elevator pitch, your 60-second infomercial, your introduction, your value proposition.

The reason it's called an 'elevator pitch' is that if you were caught in an elevator with someone and you only had a minute to introduce yourself and tell them what it is you do, what would you say? It's important to have a prepared script to tell the other person what you do, to take advantage of the potential that they could turn out to be a prospect or know somebody who could do with your help.

Remember, your prospects are only interested in themselves and not you or your services. So what's in it for them? What are the benefits to them? What are they looking for? What do they want?

Take a look at the pains and the wants of your prospects that you identified in the earlier exercise. So with all the information that you have through the other exercises, now work though **Exercise 21** to put together your value proposition.

I've included two different sets of questions to give you two options for an elevator pitch. What you need to do is answer the questions and fill in the blanks. In this way, you can choose what works for you and bring your own style to the conversation.

Here's an example of mine:

My name is Paul Davis, and I work with people in professional services – accountants, solicitors, coaches and consultants – to help them get more clients, more fees and more time. I've tripled the fees of people I've worked with, which means they have more money to build their wealth and not worry about struggling with cashflow.

The important thing, however, is to make sure you have a sequence prepared and have tried verbalising it a number of times so that it comes naturally to you when it's time for you to introduce yourself to somebody. The last thing you want is to be stumbling over your words and leaving them with the impression that you don't know what you do.

Exercise 21 – Your USP

My USP...

My name is:

Who I do it for:

What I do is:

Why me:

The value I provide is:

Alternative:

You know how some ... (your target market)

Experience the challenge ...

Which means that ...

Well, what I do is ...

Which means that ...

The benefit of which is ...

WHERE'S THE WATERING HOLE?

Can you picture being on safari in an African plain, and all around you are elephants, zebras, giraffes ... you can probably even hear them and the noises they make.

Where do all the animals travel long distances to?

They all have to come to one place. They instinctively know where to go, and they come here in their droves (herds!). They all have to come to one place to find water: the watering hole.

The water stays there; it doesn't move. It always appears in the same place no matter what. And the water doesn't have to do anything. It just has to be water. It doesn't have to change its colour or appearance, or jump up and down, make noise or advertise itself.

Where is the watering hole for your niche market?

No matter what niche market you want to provide your services to, there's always a watering hole for the people in it. There's always a place where they congregate, meet, share ideas, learn new things, meet their peers, read their industry magazines, are regulated by a particular body ... Where is their watering hole?

You will recall earlier in the book I referred to doing a search in Google for petroleum companies, which showed the conferences, associations, specific reports, etc. for that niche. The same applies to your niche.

In **Exercise 22**, work through all the places where your niche congregate so that you have identified all the places that they go to.

Exercise 22 – The Watering Holes

The watering holes for my niche are ...

Once you've identified where the watering holes are, your aim is now to put yourself in the centre of each of those watering holes. When you're in the centre of their watering holes, they'll come to you. You'll become known as the expert in your field, in their industry. And once you're at their watering hole, what do you do?

I'm sure you've spent years becoming qualified in your field, getting the experience and gaining all the knowledge that you have. And I'm sure you've spent €000s in the process.

So if anybody wants to get any of your experience or knowledge, surely they have to pay for it? Why give them any information until they have paid for it?

Right?

Well ...

WHAT'S YOUR BIRD SEED?

Do you remember when you were a child and you went to the park? And when you got to the park, you could see a group of birds gathered around on the ground picking up the crumbs that people left behind? And your reaction was to go chase the birds and catch them, just because it's great fun?

So what do the birds do when they're chased? They fly away.

You see, a lot of the time service professionals go chasing their prospects. But if you're chasing, what are your prospects doing? They're running away!

But what does the wise old person do to get the birds to come to him or her? He just sits there on the park bench and holds out his hand. And in doing so, he takes some bird seed or bread crumbs and places it on the palm of his hand.

What begins to happen? The birds start to fly to his hand and take the bird seed.

Some of us, however, want to keep our packet of bird seed in our pocket and not even open it for fear that the birds might go away with it all. After all, we've paid so much for the bird seed (our knowledge) and it's taken so long for us to gather it in the first place. So why would we give it away free?

But, you see, after the birds come and take the bird seed, what do they do? They fly off and tell their friends, "Hey, Charlie, there's loads of free food over there. Pass the word along and get everybody to come to where the food is". And their friends tell their friends, who in turn tell their friends. And you're in the centre of their watering hole, aren't you?

You see, as a professional in your field, you're extremely lucky. The reason being there's never an end to the amount of knowledge you have and will continue to have. I could write several books about business development for professionals and I still wouldn't have exhausted my knowledge. Take, for example, everything that I'm including in this book, or even just take this concept of bird seed – I'm explaining what you need to put in place, the reasons why, and what bird seed is. But I could write another book just about how to create your bird seed, what elements you absolutely must have in your bird seed in order to make it work, what its structure is, what language and tone you use along with all the other elements that you need to consider when creating your own bird seed. So you see, you will never run out of the knowledge as a professional service provider that will be of value to your clients.

If there's no bird seed, what happens? No birds appear. You must place yourself in the middle of their watering hole and give out your bird seed! All you have to do is figure out what piece of bird seed you can put out on your hand so that your prospects (sorry, I mean the birds) can come and take it away.

And you know, this bird seed can take many forms. You just need to package it. You don't even have to hold your hand out, you can put it out on your bird table: your website, your social media profiles, your business card, your marketing materials.

Brainstorm a few different things that you can do to put some bird seed out in **Exercise 23**.

Exercise 23 – Your Bird Seed

What's my bird seed going to be? What are my target clients looking for? What knowledge can I provide them with?

What way will I provide my bird seed?
- eBooks
- Videos
- Podcasts
- Special Reports
- DVD
- CD
- Other?

THE TEAPOT ...

Now let me tell you the difference between a service and a product and how this difference affects your clients' buying decisions.

Imagine your client buys a teapot and takes it home. He then goes to make himself a pot of tea and begins to pour it into a cup. But, for some reason, the teapot leaks. There's something wrong with it.

What does he do with the teapot he's just purchased?

The next day he takes it back to the shop, and looks for a refund or a replacement. When a client buys a product, if there's a fault with it, he can always take it back to get a refund or a replacement at no extra cost to him. But more importantly, in the client's mind, the blame for the fault lies with the supplier or the manufacturer. The blame for the fault never lies with the client themselves.

The contrary, however, applies to when it comes to a service. If there's something wrong with a service that a client receives, while the client may complain to the service provider, there is often little that can be done to rectify the situation by way of getting a refund or replacement. While the client may get a refund, part of what goes on in their mind is that they go through all the 'should haves':

- I should have done more research;
- I should have done more reference checks;
- I should have talked to other service providers;
- I should have talked to previous clients, and so on.

So, in relation to services, the client is naturally cautious and doesn't want to mess things up by picking the wrong service provider.

So how do you get around this? Simple ...

YOUR FIRST SALE ...

Always make your first sale a low price sale!

Have something that you can offer to your prospects that is at a low price to them. In this way, they are then entering into a buying routine and their risk is extremely low. They can test you out, see whether they like you, and if they do, then they can go for the bigger buys you have to offer. But at least you have the opportunity to start a relationship with that client and prove to them that you're of benefit to them.

Many professionals only sell their BIG service. But look at how many clients they are turning away as a result. The risk is too high for potential clients to invest in the big purchase without knowing enough about them and whether they can deliver.

In **Exercise 24**, try and figure out what you can offer your prospects that would be a low price first sale.

Now a lot of professionals tell me, "If I can just get in front of the prospect. I'll be OK. I can convert them into a client".

Why not have it the other way around?

Why waste your time chasing after clients, when you can spend your time better serving the clients you already have?

By having your bird seed out on the table, in the centre of your niche watering holes, you'll be presented with hundreds of opportunities for your prospects to buy your low price first sale and road-test you before going for the big price ticket.

Exercise 24 – Your Low Price First Sale

What can I offer my prospects as a low price first sale?

YOUR CLIENT JOURNEY ...

Let's turn our attention to how your client or your prospect interacts with you. This is called your 'client journey'.

Have you ever walked into a hotel and seen empty cups and glasses on the tables in the reception area? Or gone up to the receptionist only to find you have to wait 10 minutes for her to acknowledge that you're even there?

It then takes a half-hour just to check in and get to your room, where you have to carry your own bags. You get to the room and you can see mould on the windows and the room looks like it hasn't been fully cleaned.

And no, I haven't stayed in poor class hotels. I could go on and on about hotels, restaurants, retail stores, but you get the picture.

What is the experience of your business like for your clients and prospects?

Take it from the first interaction – it may be your website (if you have one!). Is it confusing, does it use their language, can they clearly see what's in it for them, does it have a display saying 'under construction'?

Then they make a phone call (if you're lucky) only to get an answering machine where they can hear children screaming or the dog barking in the background on the message. The phone call is returned three days later (or not at all), when they've forgotten why they rang in the first place.

These are not exaggerations and I'm sure you've experienced situations like that yourself in various different ways and with various different service providers.

Sometimes, we believe we're doing our best and that we provide a very professional service. But have you ever road-tested your client journey from your clients' eyes as opposed to from your own eyes? Have you ever asked yourself what people generally say about your profession as a whole and the typical service that people get from such a profession?

Common reactions that I get when I pose this question to groups of people are:

- For solicitors: expensive; always on the clock; and they never return phone calls!

- For accountants: they're not helpful; I only see them once a year; I have to ask them for something that I want rather than them telling me what I need to know for my business.

Now I don't mean to offend anybody or any profession, after all I'm an accountant myself. But just ask any group of people at your next networking meeting and see what they think of your profession (not you personally). You'll be shocked at what they'll tell you and most of the time you won't believe it.

However, look at what you can do by being armed with that information. Consider the difference you could make to how you yourself are portrayed and the systems you can put in place to counter each one of those comments. If you did this and your clients could see the difference, what do you think they'll be saying to their friends and associates?

I once asked one of my clients to do this exercise. She ran a large garden centre. So she decided to take her car down the road and with her 'client's hat' on decided to observe what clients saw. What she noticed was the lack of signage approaching the nursery. It was difficult to find as it was not on the main road, and the trees and hedging on the approach weren't the most appealing. Next she drove into the car park and parked her car, and immediately in front of her was a stack of fertiliser! Not the most beautiful sight to see when you first arrive. The list went on and on, but it gives you an idea of what you need to look out for. Needless to say, she moved the fertiliser to another place and replaced it with a tall display of bedding plants that were in full colour. And she went on to improve the approach and erect signage.

It is worth mapping out in **Exercise 25** the step-by-step journey that your clients take. Starting at the beginning, right through to your office, your stationery, your service, your invoice, your payment collections system, your after-sales service, your follow-up. All the way through every touch point that your client will encounter with you and your business.

Then ask yourself how each of these steps could be improved, even slightly. Because a number of small improvements along the way will make a massive difference in total to your clients.

Exercise 25 – Your Client Journey

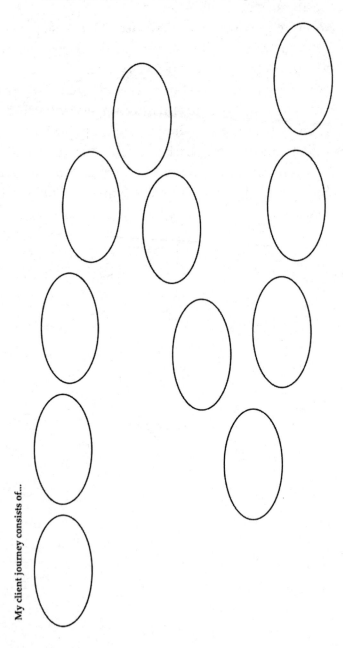

My client journey consists of...

Action items I can take to improve areas of my client journey are...

TESTIMONIALS ...

The normal reaction I get from people when I first suggest that they start collecting testimonials is one of "But I hate them", or "They're not worth the paper they're written on".

Sound familiar?

But let me ask you this question: Have you ever read testimonials? You may not have read them for the purpose of allowing them to change your mind (you think!), you may have just read them for curiosity. No matter, you still read them.

However, remember what I said earlier about the teapot. People need to see testimonials as part of their building up knowledge about you and the results you get for your clients before they engage with you. Unconsciously, they need to see that other people have purchased your service and are happy to recommend you. It's part of the way they gather all the information to convince themselves that they're making the right decision.

And because you provide an excellent service, then there's no reason why your current or past clients won't give you a testimonial.

Now when you're asking your clients for a testimonial, there is absolutely no point in simply asking them, "Would you be able to give me a testimonial?".

What happens when you ask this?

They of course say "Yes", but then you never receive it. The reason is that many people don't know what to write in a testimonial. Therefore they never start to write one and hence you don't receive it.

Some clients might say to you, "Sure, you write it and I'll sign it". The problems with this approach are that:

- The testimonial is not written in the language that your client uses;

- You might be missing something very important that was of value to your client; and

- It won't be authentic.

So how do you get around this?

Well here's a sequence of questions that you can ask:

- *Question 1 – Can you remember what it was like before we started working together – on your accounts, business, legal case?* This gets them back to what it was like for them and the pain they were in.

- *Question 2 – Out of all the work we have done together, what do you feel was of the most benefit to you?* This gets your client to think about one thing that was important to them.

- *Question 3 – What difference did it make to you to have this* (insert whatever your client responded with to the previous question)*?*

Once you have closed off on these questions and your client has given you enough to work with, acknowledge your appreciation for their generous comments and feedback. You can then ask them if they would be OK for you to use what they said as part of your marketing materials provided you send them a copy of the testimonial first.

In this way, you're in control of writing up the testimonial, but it's in their words, and it's genuine. Second, by asking these questions, you find out what was of the most value to your clients. This will help you in developing your service with other clients but also you will be amazed as to what they will say.

So let's list out all the people you can approach who will give you a testimonial or a recommendation.

Exercise 26 – People For Testimonials

People I will approach for a testimonial include ...

ACRES OF DIAMONDS ...

Now at this stage, you have a lot of work completed and you've probably even started implementing some of the ideas in your own business following the exercises you've carried out so far, and are seeing the benefits already in your business.

I want to cover with you another area of your business that needs to be worked on: what activities you're going to do to market yourself.

But first I want to outline something you may have come across previously: Acres of Diamonds.

The book, *Acres of Diamonds*, is one of the most famous books in the world. The author, Russell Conwell, was asked to give a speech to the 10-year reunion of the Civil War troops. He gave this speech, 'Acres of Diamonds'. Afterwards, it was requested over and over again throughout the years.

It is fair to say this speech probably was given more times than any other speech in the history of the world. Russell Conwell personally gave this speech over 6,000 times, travelling from city to city. With the proceeds from giving the speech, he would pay for his room, board and train fare, and then send the rest back to Temple University. These funds put nearly 2,000 students through college.

The book details story after story of people overlooking riches in their own back yard, only to spend their time looking elsewhere.

Most people under value what they know. Most people think of themselves as ordinary and accept ordinary incomes and outcomes.

Once people are made aware of the value of what they know, they go on to be much more successful. Once people wake up to the possibilities of finding opportunities, they start to see them everywhere.

You can get a free copy of *Acres of Diamonds* by visiting this website: **http://www.davisbusinessconsultants.com/resource-library/downloads/.**

There are many interpretations and ideas that you'll get from the book and it is therefore worth reading it a number of times.

The main purpose of the story, however, and the reason why I'm bringing it up here is to highlight the fact that a lot of the time we spend an enormous amount of time and effort searching and looking for new clients in far-off places, when in fact there are plenty of clients (diamonds) on our door-step.

The easiest way to get more clients or more business is by looking at the clients you already have, and past clients.

These are people who already know you well, they're happy with the service you provide, and you don't have to sell yourself to them again. They can do the selling for you!

So ... we're going to look at how you can get referrals.

YOUR REFERRAL SYSTEM ...

Many of the professionals I work with didn't have a referral system in place, and many of those that did, had one where they would simply ask their clients something along the lines of "If you know of anybody that is looking for X, it would be great if you could mention my name to them".

Does this sound familiar?

Do you agree that it is easier to get business from people we already know? Do you agree that it is easier for your clients to explain the benefits of your service to other people? Do you agree that other people will listen to a recommendation from people that they already have a relationship with and trust?

Then ... it's time for you to put a referral system in place. By this I mean a systemised approach that you adapt to asking for referrals. Very much like you have a systemised approach for getting up in the morning, getting ready for work, and then getting into your car to get to your office. You approach it pretty much the same way every time and you do it automatically without having to think about it.

So the first thing you need to do is to set milestones in your client journey (we spoke about this earlier) where you ask for referrals from your clients. Most people, if they ask for referrals, ask for them after they have delivered their service. I'm going to ask you to look for referrals a number of times during your client journey.

Let me explain ... have you ever heard the term "eaten bread is soon forgotten"? What it means is that your hunger desire quickly passes away as soon as you've eaten the bread.

Take your client. When they come to you, they have a real problem (hunger). A client of a solicitor, for example, may want to get a legal letter sent out to one of their suppliers as quickly as possible. An accountant's client may have just received a letter from the taxman and they need to get the problem sorted quickly. A physiotherapist's client may have a leg injury that is really paining them.

Do you get the picture? Do you think they are in a state where they want to get something sorted quickly? Their need is high.

Do you think that a few months down the road after you've delivered your service that they'll have forgotten the pain they were in when they first approached you to help them out?

Do you think they will really remember all the work you did to help get rid of their pain? Hence the reason for asking for referrals earlier – eaten bread is very soon forgotten when it comes to delivering a service.

Well then ... let's start by putting a system in place where you'll systematically ask for referrals. Take a look through your client journey in **Exercise 25** and pick the points where it suits you best to ask for a referral. Then in **Exercise 27**, write out the points at which you're going to ask for referrals.

Exercise 27 – Your Referral System

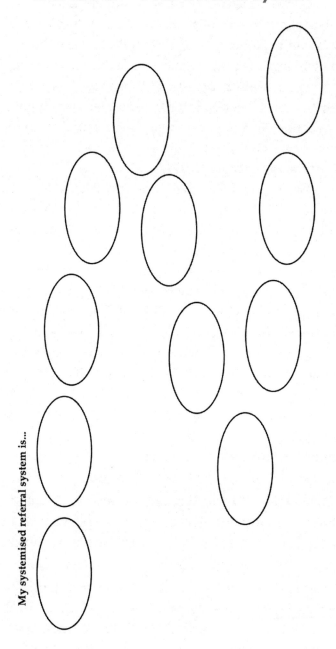

My systemised referral system is...

When you have done this, write in beside the points *how* you're going to ask for the referrals. This may be by way of face-to-face meetings you're going to have, by email or by telephone.

Are there any documents that you use when working with a client that you need to update so that there is a reminder for yourself to ask for referrals? For example, you might have a 'client meeting agenda' or 'engagement letter' or other such documents that you use. If there is, write a note in the exercise sheet to make the changes to those documents.

Now ... we're going to look at how you ask for referrals.

As I said earlier, many people ask along the lines of "If you know of anybody that is looking for X, it would be great if you could mention my name to them".

This is completely the wrong way of asking for referrals. Your clients have no idea what to look for and, as soon as you're out the door, they've forgotten about it. The majority of people ask for referrals in this way so it's as meaningless as asking them what time of day it is. Our brains aren't designed to answer wide-ranging questions such as this: "If you know of anybody...".

You have to do the work on behalf of your client so that their brain can process what exactly you are looking for. Your referral script needs the following structure:

Let's use an example of a business owner:

- *Question 1 – How long have you run your own business?* The purpose of this question is so that your client can go to the filing cabinet in his mind to access the file 'my business'.

- *Question 2 – I suppose, over the years, you've probably met a number of other business owners, haven't you?* This now opens the 'business owners' file within that same cabinet. The 'suppose' and 'probably' softens the question to make it easier to answer. The 'haven't you' prompts a "Yes" answer.

- *Question 3 – If I asked you to write down the names of, say, two or three of those people, you could probably do that, couldn't you?* This now gets the client to pick the two or three people out of their 'business owners' file that come to mind straight away. The 'If' indicates that you're not asking the question. You're only asking 'if'. The 'two or three' indicates that the client has a choice. The 'probably' softens the question. And the 'couldn't you' prompts another "Yes" answer.

- *Question 4 – So, would it be OK if I contact them?* This results in getting a "Yes" answer before you even state the reason why you want the names.

- *Question 5 – May I ask your advice?* This enables a "Yes" answer.

- *Question 6 – Of the people you're thinking of, who should I contact first to let them know how they can benefit in the same way you have benefited from us working together?* This is where you're asking for the names of the referrals. The 'first' indicates you want more than one referral. Now take the details and prompt for the 'second, third ...'.

- *Question 7 – To make it easier for these people to take my call, is it OK for me to use your name?* The use of 'easier for these people' infers that it won't be a hassle for the people you'll be contacting.

So there you have it ... seven easy steps to getting a lot more real referrals.

You may choose not to ask all the questions, depending on your relationship with your client, but what needs to be kept in mind is doing the work for your clients so that they can identify people in their own mind. For example, what other accountants do you know well?

What you are best off doing now is to write out your own script so that you can practice it and put your own terminology onto it.

In **Exercise 28**, write out your questions using the structure above.

It's always good to use a referral form. In this way, you can then give the form to your client to fill out or you can send it to your clients along with a covering letter. This form would just have spaces for your client to fill in the contact details of people they are happy for you to talk to.

The main thing I want you to do is to start asking for referrals in a better way and to have a system in place for asking for referrals.

You can also state to your client upfront when you begin working with them that, at various points in your business relationship with them, you will be asking for referrals to other 'business owners' that they know.

In this way, you are making them aware of what you will be doing and it also highlights how confident you are about the service you provide and the benefits that they will get.

Exercise 28 – Your Referral Script

My referral script is...

Question 1

Question 2

Question 3

Question 4

Question 5

Question 6

Question 7

STAYING IN TOUCH ...

When you look back at the hundreds of people that you've met over the years, how often do you keep in touch with them all?

And when you go to a networking meeting, what do you do with all the business cards afterwards?

Typically they're kept in a drawer somewhere in your office.

You can't make a phone call to all those people every month to keep them updated on what you're doing or any new services you're providing. And you can't take them all out to lunch as this would cost you a fortune and you'd get nothing done.

But ... if you're not making regular contact with these people how will they remember you?

I'm sure that when I asked you earlier to look back and remember the hundreds of people that you've met over the years, you had forgotten some of the many people you had met.

Imagine if you were able to keep in contact with all the people that you've met over the years and keep them updated as to what you are doing. Not only them, but also all the people that they know who could do with your service.

But if you're not keeping them updated, how will they remember you?

So, the first thing you need is a way of keeping track of all the people that you meet. You can buy a really sophisticated client relationship management (CRM) system, but starting off you can manage with a simple spreadsheet or file. Then as your database begins to grow, you might look at software that will handle a lot of the work for you. But at least you will know at that stage what you want the system to do for you and how best you want to use it because you will have tested out your own manual system first.

In **Exercise 29**, list out all the details you want to keep for the people you come in contact with.

Exercise 29 – Your Contact Database

My contact database will consist of the following details:

Name

Email address

Telephone

Company name

Company address

Other useful information

How am I going to maintain a database of my contacts?

There are many systems available online. If you want to take a look at an online CRM system that you can use for free and test out before you upgrade to a paid for version, take a look at either of these links:

- http://www.highrisehq.com/
- http://www.constantcontact.com.

Now that you have an idea of how you're going to maintain a database of these contacts, what are you going to do to keep in contact with them on a regular basis?

It's best if you classify them into two different groups of people:

- Group A – the top say 10% to 20% of people that you want to keep in contact with in a more personal way;
- Group B – maybe the 80% to 90% of people that you want to keep in contact with by using an automated system.

There are a number of ways you can keep in contact with your first group, including:

- Phone calls;
- Personalised emails or letters;
- Face-to-face meetings;
- Going to events or seminars together;
- Mastermind groups;
- Research teams.

For Group B people, you may decide to keep in contact with them in any one of the following ways:

- Printed newsletter;
- Electronic newsletter;
- Business events;
- Social events;

- Research programmes;
- Market summaries;
- Book reviews.

What other ways can you think of to keep in touch with your contacts? In **Exercise 30**, clearly identify the method(s) you'll adapt to stay in touch with your contacts and brainstorm several topics that you can use as content for your newsletters, events or programmes.

By now, you can see that, by having a clearly defined niche market to focus on, where you're demonstrating key benefits to that market at their watering holes and by having some bird seed to offer them, they can then test your low price first sale to start building trust with you, and by having a system of staying in touch and constantly looking at your client journey to see where improvements can be made, and by having a systemised referral process, you're going to be well on the way to getting more clients.

But we're not finished yet!

There's plenty more to help you.

Exercise 30 – Your System of Staying in Touch

My system for staying in touch will be...

The topics I'm going to cover will be...

THE MATRIX ...

No, I'm not referring to the film of the same title here!

A common problem I come across often when working with professionals and their client relationships is that their clients don't know what they do.

Let me explain ... John is an accountant. He's been working with a particular client, Mary, for years, preparing her annual accounts. One day during a meeting with Mary, she starts to describe how she came across another professional, Michael, who is going to come in and review her business strategy with her management team. While John is listening to Mary's story, he's saying in his own head, "How many times have I told her that I could do that for her?". But it's too late now, he can't say anything as Mary has already engaged Michael to run the first workshop with the team.

Does this scenario sound familiar to you in your line of business? Have you ever had a time when a client of yours has turned to you and said that they've engaged somebody else to carry out some work that you know you could have carried out and earned those fees?

You see, you may have told your client hundreds of times but it wasn't in a language they understood. Remember I spoke earlier about the fact that your clients only tune into one radio station: WIIFM. You need to tell them in their language – tell them the benefits that they can understand rather than giving them a shopping list of your services. And you need to tell them on a regular basis as part of your system of staying in touch.

I call this systematic approach 'doing your matrix'. It's a simple spreadsheet where, on one side, you list out all the different services you provide, perhaps in a row going across the top. Then on the other side, in a column down the left, you list all the clients you currently work with and all the clients you've worked with in the past. Then you start to fill in the boxes between both of these axes, to identify which clients have purchased which services.

You can see an example of what this looks like in **Exercise 31**.

When you're finished, you'll be able to see immediately which of those clients haven't purchased your full range of services.

Now because you already have a relationship with these clients, you can very easily have a system in place where you inform them on a regular basis of the different services you provide.

You can't give your clients a full list of your services all at once, since it's going to appear like a shopping list. So what you need to do is wrap them up in a case study or a story that you can tell your client in order to give them an example of how the situation arose for another client and how you were able to solve their problem. In this way, your client will be able to identify themselves with that problem and know that you're the person to solve it for them.

Work through **Exercise 31** to see where the gaps arise in your own business and put in place a system where you can systematically make all your clients aware of the services they have not yet bought from you.

And remember the story about *Acres of Diamonds*, why look for more clients when you already have a field of clients at your doorstep and you can easily gain new business from them?

Exercise 31 – Your Matrix

Sample Client Matrix

Client	Service				
	A	B	C	D	E
Client 1	X		X	X	
Client 2		X			
Client 3		X			X
Client 4			X		
Client 5				X	
Client 6				X	
Client 7	X	X			
Client 8					X
Client 9			X		

My Client Matrix

Client	Service				
	A	B	C	D	E

YOUR MARKETING ACTIVITIES ...

Now what do you currently do to make people aware of your services?

The answers I typically get to this question are:

- "I attend networking events"; and
- "I advertise in the *Golden Pages / Yellow Pages*".

And that's pretty much it.

Some professionals don't even have business cards, and many that have them don't carry them around with them everywhere. Does this sound familiar?

What use are your business cards if they're stuck in a drawer somewhere? You've already paid to get them printed, so why not hand them out to everybody you meet?

And have you ever met somebody who hands you their business card and then they say, "It needs to be updated. I've changed my telephone number / my email address".

What does this say to you?

Professional? Not quite. So let's look at this for a minute.

Do you remember we covered your sales funnel, and we identified the number of people you need to be talking to on a regular basis in order for you to achieve the income target that you've set?

Well, if you were to double the number of marketing channels you currently have, what difference would that make to your business? How about if you were to add a new marketing channel to your business each month? This would mean that you would have 12 new marketing channels this time next year.

Add these 12 new marketing channels to your existing channels, and having done the previous exercises and the fact that you have a clearly defined niche market to focus on, where you're demonstrating key benefits to that market at their watering holes, and by having some bird seed to offer them, they can then test your low price first sale to start building trust with you, and by having a system of staying in touch and constantly looking at your client journey to see where improvement can be made, and by having a systemised referral process, then you can see how with these systems you will be able to have a steady stream of clients for your business.

So let's continue ... I've listed out below some of the different marketing activities that you can do to increase the awareness of your services in the market that you're operating in. Go through this list and identify the marketing channels that you're going to adapt for your business:

- Networking;
- Telemarketing;
- Speaking / lecturing;
- Website (own / other people's);
- Newsletter;
- Live seminar;
- Teleseminar;
- Podcast;
- Write articles / books / eBooks;
- Client reviews;
- Referral system;
- Low price first sale;
- Guarantee;
- Affiliates;
- Focus groups;
- Free resources / guides;
- Word-of-mouth tool;
- eCourses;

- Taster sessions;
- Google ads;
- Event host;
- Alliance partners;
- Blog;
- Mailshots;
- Own database;
- Sponsorship;
- YouTube videos;
- Social networking;
- Business cards;
- Mobile SMS texts;
- Agents;
- LinkedIn;
- Audio CDs;
- Bonuses;
- Email marketing;
- Source from existing clients;
- Exhibitions;
- Postcards;
- Webinars;
- Radio;
- Road shows;
- Yellow Pages;
- Advertising / PR;
- Video mailing.

Then go to **Exercise 32**, write in the marketing channels you're going to adapt and add any more you can think of.

Exercise 32 – Your Marketing Channels

My Marketing Channels...

Now that you have the marketing channels that you're going to adopt, go to **Exercise 33** and put an X under the month that you're going to have each of the channels in place by.

Exercise 33 – Your Marketing Plan

My marketing plan....

Marketing Activity	Month											
	1	2	3	4	5	6	7	8	9	10	11	12
1												
2												
3												
4												
5												
6												
7												
8												
9												
10												
11												
12												

FEAST AND FAMINE ...

A lot of professionals go through what I call a 'feast and famine' revenue cycle.

By this I mean, that when a service provider is in the famine part of their revenue cycle, they go out and do a lot of marketing activity and this brings in business. And behold they have a feast!

And now that the business is coming in, they take their foot off their marketing pedal, which in time leads to a famine again.

So then they go out and do a lot of marketing activity and this brings in business. And behold, they have another feast! But now that business is coming in again, they take the foot off their marketing pedal again ... you get the picture!

Have you ever noticed this in your own business?

In order to get consistent revenue results, you have to do a level of marketing all the time, even when you're busy. The marketing activities you've identified earlier need to be set up in such a way that many of them are automated so that they happen without you having to spend a lot of time each week on making sure they're generating leads for you.

We'll talk a little later about managing your time but, for now, I want you to start thinking about having your systems in place where you're continuously doing marketing. This is one of the main reasons so many professionals find themselves with little or no clients because they've been spending all their time concentrating on a few particular clients and when those projects have finished, they have to spend a lot of time generating new business.

By keeping your marketing activity going on a consistent basis, you will have a steady stream of clients coming your way.

PRICING YOUR SERVICES & WINNING THE BUSINESS

PRICING YOUR SERVICES ...

Now we've looked at the services you're going to provide, and identified the market in which you're going to provide those services to meet the needs of your prospects. And we've also looked at how you're going to market those services and get in front of your prospects, so now let's take a look at how you're going to price your services and win the business.

This is such an important area and one that many professionals miss out on.

Many professionals well under-price their services when they start their own business. They aim low in their expectations of the revenue they could achieve.

If you want to operate on a 'time spent' basis – to charge by the hour or day – here is an exercise you can work through in order to determine the hourly rate you should be charging.

Take your last annual salary and, to make it easy, let's say it was €100,000. Even though there's 52 weeks in the year, you've got to allow for your own holidays and public holidays. So let's say we're now down to a realistic 48 weeks in the year.

The average productivity of a solo-professional is about 48% in the first four years of business. This means that you're productive (charging time) for only 48% of your time. The rest of the time is taken up in setting up the business, marketing, administration, meeting prospects, dealing with day-to-day issues as they arise etc.

So in order to earn the same level of income of €100,000, your weekly charge out rate would be:

€100,000 annual salary / 48 weeks in the year = €2,083.33 per week.

Knowing that there are five working days in the week, this rate would then become:

€2,083.33 / 5 actual working days = €416.66 per day.

And working at 48% productivity, your charge out rate would then become:

€416.66 per day / 0.48 productivity = €868.04 per day.

And if you're going to charge on an hourly basis, this will mean your charge out rate will be:

€868.04 / 7 hours per day = €124.01 per hour.

So that's how you work out what your charge out rate should be per hour / day.

But that rate is before you start taking into account the cost of office space, equipment, staffing, running costs, etc. that also need to be added.

However, what are the implications of pricing your services in this way? Some of the implications typically are:

- Your client will get 'hung up' with your hourly rate and will look to get it reduced;

- It's easier for people to compare your rate with that of the competition and this forms a natural progression to competing on 'rate';

- For the client, it then becomes more of an issue to them to find out how many hours you will work for them and how long the project will take;

- For you, it will mean having to keep track of hours worked and time billing;

- What then happens to travel time to and from your client – is this chargeable?

- It potentially leads to you working longer hours than you would normally take in order to have sufficient chargeable hours;

- The focus becomes more about the hours billed rather than the value for the client.

More important, however, is that an hourly rate imposes a ceiling on your earnings.

By that I mean that in order for you to earn more fees in a year, you have to either increase your charge out rate or increase the number of hours you work.

So let's look at a way that you can double or triple (if not more) your fee income, without having to take on more staff.

PRICING BY VALUE ...

Do you believe all clients should be charged the same rate for your time?

Do you believe your clients benefit from your services in different ways? Do you believe that the same service to one client could benefit them in one way, and the exact same service to another client could benefit them in a much greater way?

Now do you think all your clients should be charged the same rate for your time?

Now you might be thinking, I'm a therapist and I can't charge my clients different rates!

Let me relay a conversation I had with a therapist on this very subject recently. She wanted to earn more fees and the only way she thought this was possible was to take on other therapists. She also knew that the therapists she was thinking of taking on wouldn't have the same level of knowledge and expertise to deal with the clients in the way that she wanted to.

So we went through the clients that she had and we were able to break them down into three categories – which you can do now in your own mind for your own clients.

Again I ask the question, do you believe your clients benefit from your services in different ways?

She was able to determine that the impact on the different categories of clients was greatly different and the benefit that they derived was vast.

As a result, she then went on to charge different rates for each category of client. So, without taking on any new staff, she was able to increase her rates substantially as a result of looking at her clients in this way.

But let's go one step further, as I just wanted to get that example out of the way for those of you who charge a rate per hour in this kind of field.

Let's now look at really pushing yourself – and I did ask you to give 100%. I want to change your mind-set completely about the way you charge fees.

I'm going to show you a strategy and, should you choose to adapt it, it will far exceed your expectations when it comes to pricing and will result in you winning more clients than if you adapt the time billing method we went through earlier.

Now I'm going to presuppose here that you want to earn more fees. If not, and you feel that earning more fees from clients is not the right thing to do for you, then that's fine. But if that's the case, it might be better to look at this structure as a way of getting your client to feel happy with the fee he or she is paying you even if you continue to charge on the same hourly basis. Both viewpoints are fine no matter which approach you take.

I come from the position that I want to make sure that the clients I work with get real value from the services I provide and therefore the return on their investment in my services far outweighs their investment.

So ... here's the secret I spoke to you earlier about how you can achieve extraordinary levels of revenue.

This is where I'll bring you through the key stages of pricing your services according to value rather than pricing on an hourly rate.

When most professionals meet with a client for the first time, the discussion generally takes the form of what the service provider can do for the client, the range of services they provide – the shopping list I referred to earlier, followed by a background of their qualifications and experience.

The focus from the professional's point of view is to close the deal and get the client on board. The majority of the meeting that takes place is based on trying to win the client and prove how much better the client would be by working with them.

However, I personally don't particularly like this format for client meetings. As I mentioned before, I want to work with clients that I can deliver real value to.

So the approach I want you to look at is to spend the majority of your meeting with the client around the area of value. I want you to ask questions and do as little of the talking as possible.

The kinds of questions that I want you to ask your clients are called open-ended questions. This means that the answer that will be given by your client cannot be a "Yes" or "No" answer. Such questions typically start with "How ...?", "What ...?" or "When ...?".

So now here's the structure I want you to adopt if you want to win more clients and have the ability to price your services accordingly.

There are five questions you need to ask at every first client meeting in order to work out the value of what it is worth to the client to have their problem solved:

- *Question 1 – How can I help you?* Or *Tell me about your business?* This will open the discussion and is your key to start building rapport as quickly as possible. Contrast this against the approach that generally takes place with self-centred laptop presentations, the history of the company, case studies, CVs of all the key consultants, etc.

- *Question 2 – What's working well at the moment?* The rush to identify problems and solutions can show a scant respect for the progress a client has already made. By taking our time with this step, we build real rapport and trust and therefore we are more likely to hear the real problems later. This also gets your client into a good mood and will offset their defences as they'll be used to entering into strong negotiating very quickly in other such conversations.

- *Question 3 – If there was one thing you could change, what would it be?* Take your time and allow them to think before answering. If the client comes up with a list, coach them gently to get to the root problem. Too often, we get so excited by the potential extent of the work, we gloss over this. This is where we help them clarify where the real root of the pain lies. If they do the analysis, there is a much greater probability that they will accept the eventual solution that they have played a part in developing. This is a critical question in the whole process and, when you have asked the question, you have to be silent until you get the answer.

- *Question 4 – If we solved this, what difference would that make?* This is where the client comes up with lots of benefits, and you write them all down – in their language. Feel free to repeat the question in several ways. Ask for the benefit of the benefit. Keep going until they cannot think of anything more. These are the reasons they will buy. This is where you are identifying the perceived value in the eye of the client. You might also choose to ask them what would happen if the problem was not solved. This is useful if you suspect you might have to help them overcome later indecision.

When you've got the answers to this question go back and ask question 3 again to see if there is anything else they would like to change. And then follow on to question 4 to define the value or benefits. Repeat questions 3 and 4 until such time as you feel you have everything the client wants. Most of the time the client hasn't done this exercise for themselves and you need to make sure you have all the problems clearly identified and coached the client through the issues so that it's clear in their mind.

When you have everything, summarise what you have discovered the client wants changed, and the value or benefit of achieving that change, then follow on with this next question.

- *Question 5 – If I could help you with that, would you be interested?* Either they are or they aren't. There is little point in spending time on a solution where there is no genuine interest.

If you've spent sufficient time building rapport with your client and have worked through this structure, by the time you get to question 5, the client will already want to do business with you.

At this stage, it is unlikely you will have to enter into negotiations on your fees. All you have to do is ask for the business.

So now that you have the structure for deriving the value from the client's perspective, now you can go through the remaining points of discussion to wrap the business up.

The remaining steps to follow are:

- Step 1 – Determine the value to the client;
- Step 2 – Propose a budget;
- Step 3 – Agree your fees;
- Step 4 – Agree how you expect to be paid;
- Step 5 – Ask for referrals.

When you adapt this approach and have agreed a fee for your services, you have the ability to get paid part of your fee upfront.

When it comes to agreeing a fee, as I mentioned before you can work on the basis of an hourly rate or a daily rate. However, the main reason for carrying out this type of value conversation is so that you can agree a higher fee – one that is based on the value that your client will derive from your services.

Let's just say you were to work on a project and you estimate that it will take you 100 hours to complete. You have a base fee by calculating the 100 hours by your current hourly rate. And this might equate to let's just say €15,000. However, from doing the value conversation, you're able to determine that the likely value to be delivered will be in the region of €1m. Do you think you could be paid a higher fee if you're able to bring about a value of €1m? Well, if you do, then you now have the possibility of agreeing this higher fee or a mechanism for how you could be rewarded for the increased value being delivered.

Some further thoughts on pricing your services according to value are that you shouldn't look at pricing your services by the value you put on yourself. Many professionals don't value themselves sufficiently. If you don't value yourself and therefore charge your clients accordingly, then you're not going to earn the high level of income that you deserve to earn.

Pricing according to value means pricing your services according to the value of what it is worth to your client if they employ you, or what it would mean to them if they didn't employ you. What would be the difference to your client?

Also when you quote a fixed fee, you no longer have to keep track of the hours that you've spent on a client and are therefore in a position to get part of your fee in advance of you delivering your services.

I know this may seem strange to a lot of professionals but all you have to do is ask. If that's the way you do business and if your client wants to employ your services, then they won't have a problem in paying you in advance.

It will also determine whether they are serious or whether they are going to mess you around when it comes to payment as you progress through the project.

Now, the other concern I get from professionals is Step 5 – where you ask for referrals. And the question that gets asked is

"Why would you ask for referrals, when you haven't even delivered your service?".

There are three reasons for this.

Remember what I said about "eaten bread is soon forgotten"? Well, it's best to ask for referrals at the point when they are exhilarated in the knowledge that they've just made a decision to employ your services so as to get rid of their pain.

Second, it sets the scene that you'll be asking for referrals as you move along your client journey and the client knows from day one that this is how you do business.

Third, what is going on in the client's mind is that they've just made a decision to engage with you. Remember what I said about the teapot? They now need to substantiate in their own mind that they've made the right decision. The best way that they can do this is by getting other similar people like them to employ your services as well.

If you follow the steps I've outlined above, you won't need to enter into negotiations with a client. If you've done it correctly, you've clearly identified yourself as a professional and have brought them through the value that they will derive from your services. When they see the value that they will obtain, compared to your fee, there are no negotiations to take place as a high return on investment can be clearly displayed.

The only thing I will say about negotiating is that it is a game. People want to enter into it because they feel they should do. And since it is a game, enjoy it. For some, it's all part of the process.

If you need to relinquish something, trade it for something else. For example, if you need to do something extra, trade it for getting paid sooner. Never give something away when you don't get anything in return.

THE DINNER PLATE ...

Let me ask you a few questions.

Imagine while you're sitting there that I'm standing in front of you holding a dinner plate. Imagine that the dinner plate I'm holding is round and has an intricate colourful design around the edge of the plate. You've got the picture in your mind?

Well, if I was to say to you that I purchased the dinner plate in my local department store, how much would you say I paid for it? €10, €20 or €30?

Let's say it would be €20.

Now imagine that I'm holding the exact same dinner plate, but instead of buying it in the department store, say I told you that I came across it at a car boot sale last weekend and I purchased it there. Now how much do you think I paid for it? €0.50, €1 or €5?

You might be saying to yourself €1.

Now, let's say I'm holding the exact same dinner plate, but I told you that I purchased it in a high-end store such as Brown Thomas, Harrods or Tiffany. Now how much do you think I paid for it? €100, €200 or €300?

The point is that the dinner plate is exactly the same no matter where I purchase it. However, what's critical is the perception of value that has been created by the price.

The final question for you then is to decide what level do you want to be playing at? If you price your services too low, what will your client perceive?

WRITING WINNING PROPOSALS ...

Many professionals spend a lot of their time writing proposals. The difficulty with this is the fact that they leave a meeting with the potential new client with the headache of knowing that they've got to put a proposal together when they get back to the office. And they don't know where to start! If you fall into this trap, then I'm going to ask you to stop doing proposals for clients.

Now this can be a very controversial subject, but the fact of the matter is why prepare a proposal when you haven't been guaranteed the business. You're not only wasting your time but also the cost of putting the proposal together.

I prefer to look at proposals as being 'confirmations of what has been agreed'.

If you have to prepare a proposal, it means that sufficient homework wasn't done during the meeting you had with the potential client to determine whether he or she has the authority to make the decision in the first place.

If you're dealing with corporate clients or Government bodies and the standard practice is for them to look for proposals, then I suggest still going through the same value conversation I outlined above and then following the format that I suggest you use below, simply because it works.

The first thing to know is that a proposal should really only be a confirmation and summary of what was discussed at your first meeting. The structure I gave you earlier for having value conversations will feed into your proposal on the assumption that you took notes throughout the meeting with your client.

If your client has asked you to prepare a proposal, don't just say "Yes" and leave the meeting. Confirm to them that you will prepare a proposal, but then follow up by asking them what they would like contained in it. When you've got them answering this question, work through a draft proposal with them.

That is, ask them how many pages should it be, one page or longer – this will determine whether they are looking for a lot of detail or just a summary. What are the main headings they want in the proposal? How many copies of the proposal do they need? Will they be distributing the proposal to other people in their company?

Most of the time the client just wants you to confirm the fee and payment structure and if there are any particular conditions they need to be aware of. They're not looking for a life history of your business.

When you've worked through the draft proposal with them, you will have a much closer relationship with them. Unconsciously, they have now made themselves part of your proposal and, if it is being compared to other proposals, there will be a higher sense of ownership on their part to your proposal.

So how do you structure a proposal?

First, start with the heading. Your heading must summarise the hot buttons that they expressed at your meeting. It won't just simply state 'accounting services' or such like. It must be in a language that they use, and refer to the pain that they want to get rid of. It must very quickly grab their attention and bring them back to the problem.

After the heading, you'll have an opening paragraph that might refer to your meeting or particular items you've enclosed with the proposal.

Then you need to have a heading called 'Summary'. In this, you will describe your overall thought processes for the proposal so that the client can get a quick synopsis of what it's all about.

The next heading is 'Current Situation'. Here you're going to describe the pain that the client is feeling by being in their current situation. It's important that you use the same words that your client described at your meeting. By doing so, you're getting the client to once again revisit the position and how desperately they want to have it sorted.

Your next heading is 'Our Philosophy'. In order to separate yourself from the crowd, this is where you're going to include a brief paragraph about your values or approach to dealing with clients. What you completed in **Exercise 6** will help you in writing this paragraph.

The next heading is 'Proposal'. In this section, you'll go into full details as to what your proposal is to solving the problems the client has.

The next heading is 'Costs'. Highlight here what the costs are, along with how you expect to get paid. Most people put the costs as the last item – this is the norm. When people receive proposals they always go to the end or the last page to find out what the cost is going to be. Therefore be different in your approach. By putting the costs here you are then going to go into the benefits that they are going to obtain from those costs.

So the next heading is 'Benefits'. Now that you've reminded them of the pains and the cost of removing those pains, you're going to go through the benefits that they're going to derive. Again you will use the language that your client used at the meeting so that he can relate to it immediately – what difference it is going to make to your client by having his problem solved.

The next heading is 'Conclusion'. In effect, this will repeat part of what you stated in the summary section above. In other words, tell them again what you've just told them.

Next – but not last – is the closing section. This won't have a heading but it's where you are going to ask for the business. Give them a call to action in order to get the business. Tell them what they need to do next in order to proceed. Don't just leave them hanging without knowing what their next action is.

Last, after your signature, put a 'Postscript', a P.S. This is an essential piece of the jigsaw.

Research shows the benefits of having a P.S. in your proposals. Look at this yourself – when you receive a letter from somebody, your sequence of reading typically will be heading, signature, P.S., costs, letter and in that order.

That's why the P.S. is so important. Your P.S. has to grab their attention to include the major benefits your client will receive and it reiterates the call to action.

HANDLING PROPOSALS ...

Now I'd like to give you a few pointers as to the best way to handle proposals so as to make sure you have the best opportunity for winning the business.

So many times while working with clients I've had situations where we have received proposals at the last minute of the deadline, some the size of a book and some looking as if the dog had chewed them. I'm not exaggerating here ... I've witnessed these things happen.

After going to all the work of preparing a proposal, take a few extra steps to really make your proposal shine out amongst the others – present your proposals brilliantly! This gets down to the quality of paper that you use, the binding and the envelope.

Here are some guidelines you can follow:

- Use paper with a minimum weight of $100g/m^2$. Better still to go higher. In this way your proposal will look good as well as feel good. Standard photocopier paper is $80g/m^2$.

- Make sure the envelope is of sufficient quality and size for your finished proposal. There's nothing worse than receiving a proposal that has been squashed into an envelope. By the time it has gone through the postal system, it's in tatters.

- Research shows that the best font to use is Verdana size 12 for your proposals as it makes it easier for people to read. The majority of people generally use Times Roman or Arial; however, these are more difficult for people to read. But you may have your own preferences.

- At your client meeting where you were asked to put together a proposal, one of the questions you need to ask is how many copies of your proposal should be submitted. Sometimes you may be only meeting one individual who will then have to present your proposal to a Board. If this is the case, it's important to know how many copies are required. The last thing you want is to go to all the work of putting a brilliant proposal together only for it to be pulled apart and photocopied for circulation to the Board. Deliver a proposal for each person that you know will be reviewing your proposal.

Now if you really want to win the business – take it in – hand-deliver your proposal personally.

I know it's not always possible but if you do take it in, it gives you the opportunity to meet with the person again and build that relationship more strongly.

Also there may be more questions prompted as a result of your proposal and your client may have thought of more questions to ask since your last meeting. This gives you the opportunity to 'bowl them over'.

If you promised to include anything with your proposal make sure you have it there – brochures, spec sheets, testimonials, list of client references. Part of the purpose of the proposal is to satisfy the client's information needs, so make sure they have everything they asked for.

Get someone else to read over your proposal. As good as the spellchecker is on your computer, it never picks up words that are in the wrong place, and it's more difficult for the person that put the proposal together to see these errors.

The most important thing is to make sure the client's name, business name and address have been spelt correctly. Make sure you copy it exactly from their business card. People can be very upset when it comes to their name being mis-spelt. You can't afford to fall at the first hurdle.

If it's appropriate, include an order form. Fill in as much detail on the order form as possible so that the client doesn't have to do too much work.

Agree with your client what the next step is – when the Board meeting will take place; when is a decision expected to be made – then organise it so that you call the client soon after that date. In this way you're in control of moving it forward.

Finally – speed stuns! What doesn't impress a client is for the proposal to be delivered just before the deadline, and yet so many professionals do this.

Make sure that, with everything that you do, you under-promise and over-deliver. If you met the client on Monday and the deadline for the proposal is Friday, make sure you deliver the proposal by Wednesday. Unconsciously, in your client's mind, it's a mark as to how you will be delivering your services, and your client doesn't want your service delivered at the last minute.

MANAGING YOURSELF

I've seen so many professional service providers working really long hours and getting stressed out, and not even earning much income.

If you want to have a really successful professional practice, first make sure you're doing something that you really enjoy doing. We covered this in the first section of this book. If you're not enjoying what you do, it will make it very difficult to make a success of it and even more difficult to be motivated when times are tough.

Second, make sure you have your eye on your vision – again, we went through this in the first section. Without keeping an eye on your vision, so many get bogged down with the day-to-day stuff and they don't realise the years passing by until it dawns on them that they've been doing the same thing for years, and haven't developed their business.

If you really want to make money, follow my advice earlier regarding pricing your services according to value. Remove yourself from the trap of hourly or daily income rates. It will mean that you'll be earning more fees with less hours.

Once you've mastered the above and everything else that we've covered so far in this book, you'll have a really successful business and will be moving quickly on to the next stage.

But, for now, there are two very important points to cover, and they are how you're going to manage your Time and your Stress.

HOW TO MANAGE YOUR TIME ...

With so much to do to keep the business going, it's easy to fall into the habit of staying in the office longer in the evening to get everything done, and even to come in at the weekends just to 'catch up'. However, no matter how much time we spend working, there never seems to be an end to the list of things that need to be done.

Working longer hours won't make a difference to the business in the long term. We know we should be doing things better, smarter, prioritising, planning, developing. We know it's the right thing to do. However, it's easier to do what we're comfortable with – working harder and longer.

It actually works the direct opposite to what we think. We think that, if we work longer hours, we'll get the work done and then we'll be able to relax. However, anybody that has followed this train of thought has never got to the point where they've nothing more to do and so now they can relax.

Working long hours will reduce your productivity, will result in fatigue and stress, and will hinder the development of your business – apart from what it might do to your family and relationships. And nothing is worth that.

So how should you manage your time? What are some of the habits you need to instil in yourself to really be productive and motivated to bring the business forward?

There are a myriad of different things you can do in order to reduce distractions, reduce spending time on emails or the Internet, procrastination and so on. However, there are a number of fundamental things that you must do in order to progress your business.

First ... your top three

Having a long 'to do' list is really only a 'wish list' of all the things you would like to get done. You can't do everything at the same time. So, out of your 'to do' list, what are the top three things you need to get done today? Ask yourself this question every day.

Tackle those items first before you get into any routine tasks.

If you get to lunchtime, and you have already done your top three items, guess what that will do for your performance?

My clients report that the top three approach gives them more control. It changes the basis for satisfaction, and it gives a regular sense of achievement and completion.

As such, it goes a long way to prevent you being overwhelmed.

Second ... say "No"

Anyone can say "Yes". Saying "Yes" is easy. People like you when you say "Yes". You avoid confrontation or argument. But your "Yes"s also account for a lot of stress, overwhelm and disappointment. If you cannot say "No", what value does your "Yes" really have?

What you need to learn is how to say "No". It may be to the charity that is taking up a lot of your time or to a relative who needs you to help them. Whatever it is, there is only so much you can do and you have to prioritise what's more important.

Sometimes you're going to have to say "No" to a client. Suppose, for example, your client asks you to have a report ready in two days' time. You know that the report will take much longer to finalise, especially with everything else that has to be done. You also know that it won't make much difference to the client if the report is delivered a few days later than the proposed date but you don't want to disappoint the client.

The best way to handle such a situation is to say, "I won't be able to have the report for you by Friday, but I will be able to have it with you by the following Wednesday. Is that OK?". In this way, your client is still getting the report; however, it's within a timeframe that you can commit to.

Remember – under-promise and over-deliver.

And know that most of the time the client's timeframe expectations are greatly exaggerated.

Third ... zone your diary

Have you ever noticed you have meetings throughout the week with a lot of time wasted in between?

The biggest shift for you to make is to 'zone your diary'. In other words, block your diary into zones for the different aspects of your job. Here are two examples:

Maria works in HR consultancy. Each day, she has three zones in her diary:

- In the morning, she attends to any issues that have come in overnight from her global clients;

- From 11am, she blocks out two hours of 'focus time' to work without interruption on project work;

- In the afternoon, she schedules meetings.

Another example: Alan works as a speaker, trainer and coach. His diary looks something like:

- He spends Monday and Tuesday with coaching clients;

- He works on his own business on Wednesday; and

- He travels to conferences and events on Thursday and Friday.

It's not a case of being rigid with the zoning. However, once you have a plan that you work to, everything gets much easier to manage.

If you have, say, two days in the week where you arrange meetings, it becomes very easy to arrange meetings with clients without messing up your week. You also can arrange to have your meetings back-to-back so that you don't waste time in between meetings. Otherwise, if your meetings are spread throughout the day, you don't have sufficient time to do any meaningful work between them.

So let's take a look at **Exercise 34** and draft a 'zoned diary' that will work for you.

It may take you a few weeks to get to a point where your new zonings are working because you may already have client meetings scheduled and projects to complete. But the sooner you start working with a zoned diary, the sooner your professional life will become a whole lot easier.

Exercise 34 – Zoning Your Diary

My Zoned diary – Draft 1

	Morning		Afternoon	
Monday				
Tuesday				
Wednesday				
Thursday				
Friday				

My Zoned diary – Draft 2

	Morning		Afternoon	
Monday				
Tuesday				
Wednesday				
Thursday				
Friday				

Fourth ... activities

There are three activities that you must be doing every week – yes, every week! – they are:

- Chargeable work;
- Marketing; and
- Administration.

By working on these three activities every week, you avoid the dreaded feast and famine cycle I spoke about earlier. It also ensures that your administration work doesn't build up.

When you were doing your first draft of zoning your diary, did you leave these activities out?

A final word on time management – there have been endless books published on the subject – you simply have to find what format works best for you.

The techniques I've described above work especially well for all the clients I've worked with in the professional services field.

Last, everything comes down to prioritising. We can all only do one thing at a time. Some things will only take a few seconds to complete, others days. But if you're in a situation of being overwhelmed, the only question you need to keep asking yourself is "What is the one most important thing that I need to be doing right now?". And you'll find the answer quick enough.

STAYING MOTIVATED ...

There are times you will find yourself under the desk screaming, "What the hell am I doing?".

Don't worry – it passes!

I said earlier that the service you provide has to be something that you enjoy. If you don't enjoy it, you may be able to cope with it, but it's going to be a lot harder.

If you've just realised that you're doing something that you don't really enjoy, then go back to the first part of this book and work through the exercises and you'll be able to put a plan together so as to develop your new practice.

Coupled with that, you must believe that you're capable of achieving what you're setting out to achieve. If you don't enjoy what you're doing and you don't believe you'll succeed, then you'll never succeed.

Remember what Henry Ford said:

Whether you think you can do it, or you think you can't, either way you're right.

Other than that, if you're a solo-professional, it can be a really lonely place. You have to keep your best foot forward in front of clients, be your own critic, do all the work, get new clients, keep the money flowing ...

But remember you're not alone. Every single person that runs their own business has those stressful moments at some point in their business life, and some more often than others. So it's especially important for you to put a support system in place in order to be able to handle those dark moments.

WHAT DO SUPPORT SYSTEMS CONSIST OF?

Family & Relationships

We can all spend a lot of time in our business. However, no matter what, your family are the most important thing in your life. Your family know you the most and you don't have to wear any masks in front of them – and they're the ones who can call you on your 'stuff'.

Nowhere else are you going to get a better support system – and the best thing is, it's free!

Make time for your family and relationships. Don't put it off. You went into business in the first place to have more time to do the things you wanted to do. Keep the promise to yourself and to them!

Coaching

I've had a coach ever since I set up in business for myself.

Why? Because I need to be accountable to somebody else and I wanted to be stretched to build my business. I want to push my business as much as possible, while achieving the things I want to achieve in life. It's easy to make excuses.

My coach is there to challenge my decisions, make sure I'm on the right path, to 'cuddle' me when things aren't going well and to give me a good kick up the proverbial when I need one. If I didn't have a coach I wouldn't have moved as quickly in my business as I have done.

If the top athletes have a coach, why shouldn't you? No matter what professional service you're in, you can see things your clients can't see, yes? Who's there to see the things about you and your business that you don't see? If you can't see your shadow, you need somebody who can watch your back.

If you don't have a coach – get one.

Exercise ...

The majority of professional services are carried out in a sitting position, at a desk, on the computer ... and if you're not getting exercise anywhere else – the walk from the office to the car doesn't exactly count as 'exercise' – where else are you planning on getting exercise in your life?

Apart from the health benefits of getting regular exercise – it makes us more productive and creative as it allows us time away from the work to come up with solutions to problems – more importantly, it keeps us motivated.

Planning ...

Professionals run their lives by their diary. We keep the appointments that are in our diaries; to not do so would simply be unprofessional. If something is in the diary, it gets done. But if something is not in the diary, it is no more than an intention.

Our task list is a list of our intentions: those things that we aspire to do in the spaces between appointments.

In your diary, is planning a task or an appointment? Isn't it extraordinary how easily we make appointments for others, but are reluctant to do so for ourselves?

In order to move your business forward, you need to plan time for thinking, reviewing and strategising:

- *Monthly* – carry out a regular review of operations. Are you on track for the quarter?
- *Quarterly* – a day away from the treadmill, perhaps even with a few trusted advisors or business friends;
- *Yearly* – an annual retreat that looks at the year ahead and decides on the personal and professional priorities.

Please take your diary out now, and make these appointments for the following year. It will change your life and your business.

And while you have your diary out, mark in the most important dates like family birthdays, anniversaries, children's school holidays and any other dates that your family really want you to be there for, like school sports days, competition days, graduation days.

Conferences & Training ...

Many professionals have to keep up-to-date with professional and legislative changes (Continuous Professional Development). This is laid down if you're a member of a professional body. Many professionals see CPD as an unwanted expense on the business and a waste of time.

However, I'm constantly looking for relevant training courses and conferences to attend, both in Ireland and in other countries. Not only is it an opportunity to network with other business owners, understand their challenges and share ideas, but if I come away with just one good idea then in my estimation it has paid for itself.

I've spent a lot of money on training over the years since starting my own business – why? Because it makes me more money – it's that simple. The more information I can gain, the more value I can bring to my clients, and therefore the more income I can generate as a result. Attending different types of training regularly gives me different ideas that I can implement in my business.

But not only that, by keeping up-to-date with the trends in various industries, you're immediately ahead of the crowd. You get to see opportunities well before the vast majority of other professionals, and you can therefore incorporate them into your business to make sure your business is ahead.

Not only that but you're constantly improving both yourself and your business.

Mastermind groups ...

Are you a member of a 'mastermind group'?

This is a group of business owners who meet on a regular basis to review their business, their challenges and their plans for the future. Not only do you get a massive support from the group but you also get the ability to see other opportunities, and the people in your group will want to help you achieve your plans. And you never know, they may know somebody who can help you with your plans.

Remember, your network determines your net worth! The people you associate with determine the income level you'll achieve for yourself. If you take the average earnings of the people you associate with and are around with the most, they are the highest earnings you'll achieve. These are the people that will drive and encourage you to reach new heights ... or will bring you down.

Have an interest ...

Apart from your business, is there anything else that you're interested in?

This can be sailing, fishing, golf, tennis – anything. For me, it has been horse riding. After years of looking and trying various sports and activities, I found the one thing that catches my attention every time. And, believe me, I've tried a lot of different things.

For me, with horse riding, you can always do better, there is always something to be perfected, and no matter what you're doing whether it be strolling, trotting or cantering, it consumes you. You can't think of anything else apart from yourself and the horse. Therefore, your mind can't be on the business.

And that's the most important thing – no matter what your interest is – it has to be something that will take your mind away from the business, even for a short period of time. It becomes a form of meditation. A lot of people speak about mindfulness and the benefits of mindfulness. An activity that consumes your full being is the best form of mindfulness in my opinion.

If you haven't found an interest yet, find one!

TAKE RESPONSIBILITY ...

I've come across a lot of negative people in my time. But did you ever notice that negative people constantly moan and only see what's wrong in the world but don't achieve a lot in their lives?

You see ... there are two sides of the fence – you can live on the side of the fence that is made up of *effect*, meaning what you have is as a result of the effect of somebody else – the economy, parents, relationships, business, legislation, the industry, the world ... or there's the other side – the *cause* side. On this side, you're responsible for everything that appears in your life.

Having this belief and living according to it gives you tremendous power. Because if it's your responsibility, then you can do something about it. You're in control.

When you know you are responsible for everything, then you start to ask questions like "What can I do ...?" or "How do I get ...?". With this mind-set, you're constantly moving forward while others are left behind still moaning about the economy or whatever else it might be.

And let me just break one belief – there's no such thing as 'the economy'. There's only your market and your clients and adapting successfully to circumstances whatever they may be.

I'm sure you've noticed that no matter what the economic conditions are, some companies always thrive and outperform their competition. Why? Because the issue is not 'the economy'. It's never 'the economy'. It's where You are and what You are doing.

So when you're on the cause side, you have full responsibility for everything. Once you're in this mind-set there's a lot you can do and there's a lot you can achieve.

We've covered a lot of different ways in which you can keep motivated in this chapter. Out of everything that we've covered, what are the activities you're going to incorporate into your life?

Go **to Exercise 35** and list them out.

Exercise 35 – Your Activities

What activities will keep me motivated?

BUILDING A TEAM

There comes a point where you'll have to start building a team of people around you.

I suggest that this is done very early on after starting your professional practice. Many professionals say to me, "I'll do it when my income level gets to a certain point and then I'll have the money to do so". The thing is that point typically never comes. The reason is we keep rationalising in our minds that we're able to cope with all the work, and that we would be better off doing the work ourselves. However, with this attitude, you limit the size you can build your business to.

Oh and here's another secret, there are people that can do things better than us! You don't even have to bring them on as full-time or even part-time staff. The best way to start is to begin with outsourcing some of your activities.

You see ... you're more valuable to your business when you're concentrating on delivering to clients the work you enjoy doing. The more time you can free up from doing work that you don't enjoy, the more money you'll make. And there are activities that we don't like doing ourselves – but equally there are people that love to do such work.

With today's technology, it has become even easier to outsource work. Let me introduce you to my virtual team so that you can get an idea of what can be done.

First, I have a virtual assistant – Susan looks after my calls, appointments, my administration, research, credit control and much more.

I have a freelance journalist who puts together all the articles that are published in magazines. John knows the best way of presenting an article for the reader. All I have to do is come up with the concept and a few points for discussion, write the main content of the article, and John does the rest to put it in a way that magazines prefer.

Aengus makes all the changes I need done to my websites.

Nicola, my graphic designer, formats eBooks and reports for me so as to give them a professional look and feel.

Andreas takes care of our garden maintenance – yes, our garden. Our garden is there to be enjoyed. Spending the full weekend to keep the garden in trim and weeded is not my idea of enjoying the garden.

I have many other people that do specific tasks that I know they are brilliant at doing. I also have a number of associates who carry out work on my behalf – trainers, consultants and coaches.

None of these people are based in my office. In fact, some of them are on the other side of the world.

So ... what are the activities you could outsource?

Go to **Exercise 36**, list out these activities and draw up a plan as to how you're going to get other specialist people on board to do them for you. Think of all the activities that you don't enjoy doing.

Exercise 36 – Your Outsourced Activities

What activities can I outsource?

CLOSING THOUGHTS

Well done! We've covered quite a lot, I'm sure you'll agree. So congratulations on making your way through this book and the exercises.

You now have a complete system for getting more clients, more fees and more time. But what's important is that, when I was writing this book, I wanted to give you as much value as possible. I wanted this book to be short, yet comprehensive enough for you to have as much as possible to help you with your business. There is nothing that annoys me more than reading a long book, getting to the end and finishing the book with the feeling that the author could have said what needed to be said in a few pages. I hope this is not the case for you in reading this book.

I've no doubt in my mind that, if you incorporate the tools and techniques that I've included in this book into your business, you will be well on the way to becoming a more successful service provider, getting more clients, more fees and more time.

There are more resources that you can download from my website and you might find my other books to be of value to you both personally and for your business.

But this is not the end; it's only the beginning. The next step for you is to put it into action.

From my experience of working with hundreds of clients over the years, I know that some people are incredibly self-motivated and have the ability to follow a plan and take consistent steps until it is accomplished. If you're one of those people, then congratulations, go ahead and get started and make sure you keep me posted of your success.

The majority of people, however, in my experience, want and need ongoing support and motivation. They need to know how to do things and be shown and guided. In an ideal world, you would have an ongoing structure that keeps you moving, holds you accountable, answers your queries and sticks with you until you accomplish what you set out to achieve.

As I mentioned before, it is important that you find a good coach. One that you respect and know can help you with your business. The way that I have found works best and achieves the best results for my clients is by using a blended approach to help them. By this, I mean a blend of coaching, mentoring and consultancy as is needed in each situation.

With coaching, you investigate with the help of the client by asking them questions as to what solution can be developed. It goes on the premise that the client has all the answers. This works extremely well when a client's beliefs need to be challenged. However, the majority of business owners and executives I've personally worked with over the years find that pure coaching is frustrating for them. There are times they just need to be shown what has to be done, and how to do it.

Mentoring is used in a situation where a client won't have all the answers themselves. In these circumstances, a mentor will guide and instruct a client as to what they need to do in their business.

A consultant on the other hand will carry out the majority of work on behalf of the client. A blended approach of all these – coaching, mentoring and consulting – will work best for you as a business owner. So when you're looking for somebody to work with you, try and find someone who uses a blend and knows how to help you so that you can get the best results for yourself and for your business.

Whatever 'next step' you opt for, don't let what you've learned in this book collect dust. You deserve to make more money. And the system I have just shared with you can help you reach that goal in exceptionally quick time. So take the next step.

I wish you every success for your future and I want to hear of your successes and what impact this book has had on you and your business.

And know this, you *can* do this. You have a power within you that will help you. If you set your mind to it and are fully committed, you will achieve the success you desire. Do what you're passionate about, and what brings you joy. Know why you are doing what you're doing and strive to be the best you can be. Help others to be successful and be of service to them, then you too will be successful.

From my core, I wish you every success in your business and also in your personal life, and I wish that you achieve all that you deserve. Until we meet again.

Here's to Your Success!

BONUS TRAINING VIDEO

I have put together a private video tutorial, just for readers of this book, that will help you to apply in your business the strategies I've covered and to fast-track your success to getting more clients, more fees and finally freeing yourself up to do all the extra things you want to get done in life.

You can get this free bonus training video at: **www.davisbusinessconsultants.com/bonus**.

RESOURCES

Determining your core values and vision:
www.thebookevolve.com.

Free resources: **www.davisbusinessconsultants.com**.

THE AUTHOR

Paul Davis FCMA FIMCA CGMA
Davis Business Consultants

Business Mentor, Non-Executive Director & Personal Advisor,
Inspirational Speaker & Author

Paul Davis is an acknowledged specialist in business leadership development and accelerating company growth, with the drive and passion to achieve outstanding results. To date, he has transformed several pan-industry enterprises into multi-million Euro successes, and has been involved in mergers, acquisitions and strategic partnerships across all industry sectors. He is gifted in assessing business situations and providing practical action-oriented support and guidance.

He is a fellow of the Chartered Institute of Management Accountants, a fellow of the Institute of Management Consultants and Advisors, and along with many other published articles and eBooks he is also the author of bestseller, *EVOLVE – Look Within Yourself For Business Success*.

You can find out more about Paul at **www.davisbusinessconsultants.com** or *via* email at **paul@davisbusinessconsultants.com**.

OAK TREE PRESS

Oak Tree Press develops and delivers information, advice and resources for entrepreneurs and managers. It is Ireland's leading business book publisher, with an unrivalled reputation for quality titles across business, management, HR, law, marketing and enterprise topics. NuBooks is its recently-launched imprint, publishing short, focused ebooks for busy entrepreneurs and managers.

In addition, Oak Tree Press occupies a unique position in start-up and small business support in Ireland through its standard-setting titles, as well training courses, mentoring and advisory services.

Oak Tree Press is comfortable across a range of communication media – print, web and training, focusing always on the effective communication of business information.

OAK TREE PRESS
E: info@oaktreepress.com
W: www.oaktreepress.com / www.SuccessStore.com.